Inhabited by Grace
THE WAY OF INCARNATE LOVE

William Daniel

FOREWORD BY PRINCE G. SINGH

D1301091

CHURCH
PUBLISHING
INCORPORATED

Church Publishing
19 East 34th Street
New York, NY 10016
www.churchpublishing.org

Cover design by Jennifer Kopec, 2Pug Design
Typeset by PerfecType, Nashville, Tennessee

Library of Congress Cataloging-in-Publication Data

Names: Daniel, William (William O.), author. | Singh, Prince G., writer of
  foreword.
Title: Inhabited by grace : the way of incarnate love / William Daniel ;
  foreword by Prince G. Singh.
Description: New York, NY : Church Publishing, [2019] | Includes
  bibliographical references.
Identifiers: LCCN 2019014608 (print) | LCCN 2019017764 (ebook) | ISBN
  9781640651913 (ebook) | ISBN 9781640651906 (pbk.) | ISBN 9781640651913
  (ebk.)
Subjects: LCSH: Spiritual life—Episcopal Church. | Spirituality—Episcopal
  Church. | Prayer—Episcopal Church. | Lord's Supper—Episcopal Church.
Classification: LCC BV4501.3 (ebook) | LCC BV4501.3 .D3599 2019 (print) | DDC
  248.4/83—dc23
LC record available at https://lccn.loc.gov/2019014608

For Janet and Bob—
for showing me *the way of incarnate love.*

Contents

Foreword

I deleted an offensive comment that a friend made from one of my recent Facebook posts. This friend has disagreed with my position on inclusivity in the past, and he and I have had a few offline conversations. However, he feels compelled to make what comes across as bullying and offensive comments every time I post my support in the form of a prayer for certain issues. It was a tough decision, and I made it not to further hurt people when they were already reeling under the disappointment of a painful and devastating conclusion. I respect my friend's differing opinion and continue to seek for us to be open to or understand each other's points of view even when we disagree. Our world is suffering from the wounds inflicted on others because of a variety of "right" and "wrong" positions, and we are increasingly dividing and separating ourselves because we demonize each other and then proceed to eliminate each other spiritually and even emotionally. In this book, Father Billy Daniel invites us to habituate grace as a welcome balm to soothe these and other wounds while also inviting us to practice accountability as the body of Christ. He breaks open scripture throughout this book to help us get back to the core of our faith where worship and ethics are intercession, blessing, gratitude, and solidarity.

John Keble, whose feast day we celebrate on March 29, was the pastoral inspiration behind the Oxford Movement. This was a movement in the Church of England that recalled the church to her sacramental heritage away from cavalier excesses. Keble was a humble country parson who called his generation with integrity and courage "to live more nearly as we pray." In his book *Inhabited by Grace,* Father Billy, an Episcopal priest serving in the village of Geneseo with a college that shares the name, calls us similarly to prayer. He believes prayer is a conversation within God that moves us liturgically and ethically from and back to this constant, even eternal conversation. It is at once a spiritual deep-dive unpacking our significant liturgical rhythms in the church and an open invitation to practice the way of love as Jesus embodies it in his incarnation. I hope you find it to be as engaging as I did.

I met Billy Daniel in 2015 when he came to the Episcopal Diocese of Rochester and became the rector of one of our parishes, St. Michael's in Geneseo, New York. He piqued my curiosity not so much because he had the "habit" of wearing his black cassock most of the time, but because he spoke earnestly, slowly, clearly, and thoughtfully, as though he were savoring cheese and tasting good wine between sentences! Upon moving to this college town with his lovely family, Father Billy was making his rounds in the community, often getting second glances because of the novelty of seeing a black-robed Episcopal priest. Before long he had initiated a three-party conversation between the college, the low-income housing community parents, and St. Michael's Episcopal Church. He helped catalyze a proposal for an interactive web of investment between the three communities involved. A mutual dance of mentoring, engagement, and steel drums was off and running as "R-kids." The drumming and engagement continue now with local lay leadership. Father Billy had helped connect some dots that priests are essentially asked to connect. He embodies what he writes about and through *Inhabited by Grace* makes this offering to the church and the world as his contribution to a three-part conversation between him, you, and God to discern for your context. I am sure some eternal dancing and drumming will emerge from this conversation.

Father Billy and I are very different. Liturgically, he is Anglo-Catholic and I am quite expansive in my liturgical proclivities and preferences. He is curious about my world in his interest in South Indian cuisine, the game of cricket, and generally how I perceive reality. I have noticed that he is curious about everyone he encounters, as you will observe when you start reading. We don't see eye to eye on everything, but we share more than enough grace and respect in the spaces between that allow us to cherish deep respect and friendship as followers of Christ. I trust Billy because of this, and I think this trust is mutual. His sense of humor is unpredictable, but well intentioned. In a short time, he has stepped up as one of the dependable leaders of our diocese. He is currently cochair of the subcommittee on Congregational Development Partnership grants, dean of the Southwest District, chair of the Commission on Liturgy, and a member of the Racial Reconciliation, Healing, and Justice Commission. The energy he embodies in keeping the discipline of physical and spiritual retreats both on the tennis court and at the Abbey of the Genesee is inspiring. I guess some of his energy must be emanating from the freshly roasted coffee he brews every day. I have had the privilege of witnessing and cherishing this work of art from the laboratory of sorts in his office. He is also an excellent chef, and the hospitality table in his family's home is real and grace-filled.

This book is accessible for beginners in faith and curious observers, as well as seasoned disciples and leaders striving to follow Jesus faithfully every day. Father Billy calls us to a new kind of rehab by calling practitioners of faith to overcome the numbing cultural norm of callous selfishness and inhabit instead the way of grace so freely given by God in Christ. The refrain I hear throughout this book is for us to be fully alive in our journey with Christ by moving forward within ourselves, inside the church, and out in the world. This creative movement is where the spirit of grace inhabits us when we are in right relationship with God, each other, and the land on which we stand and move and have our being. May this book be to you the blessing it was to me by its encouragement, scriptural core, poignant and accessible stories from a variety of worlds, and a joy that holds it together graciously.

The Rt. Rev. Prince Grenville Singh
Episcopal Diocese of Rochester

Preface

If you set sail from England to America crossing the Atlantic, you soon learn that the wind patterns and ocean currents do not favor a direct route from coast to coast. Rather, if you attempt to travel straight across, as the early settlers would discover after much wreckage, the wind currents and the North Atlantic Gyre[1] fight against boat and sail, compromising the expedition. However, if you travel with the Canary Current and the Gyre down the coast of Africa along the Canary Islands, and then up the coast of South America along the Bahamas, you find more favorable winds and waters that carry you along your journey. In other words, if you move with the winds and waters your trip will be more peaceful and you might actually reach your destination.

In many respects, this book is about the patterns of life that move us along peacefully toward our destinations, while naming those winds and waves that thwart us along the way. I set out to write a book about liturgy for laypersons and clergy alike that takes a fresh look at what it means to do liturgy together. It has become much more than this. It's still a book about liturgy, but it's about liturgy as a conversation. As I wrote, I continued to discover liturgical wind patterns, gyres of worship if you will, that we often overlook in our attempt to *arrive* at the coast of peace. I began wondering about prayer as something we are caught up into, rather than something we say or do. I began noticing how wrong I've been about prayer all this time, and the human tendency to pray as if sailing against the gyres of God.

---

1. A gyre is a giant circular oceanic surface current.

Here's what I've learned: we tend to think of prayer as petitioning God for things we need or giving thanks to God for blessings received, or, with little confidence that God is listening, we resolve to pray so that we can at least feel a little better about the state we're in. What if prayer is not about this at all? Don't get me wrong. We should cry out to God. We should give thanks to God. Prayer, hopefully, does have peaceful side effects. Nevertheless, prayer is more analogous to listening in on a conversation happening *within* God that by grace is flowing around us, passing between us, even stirring up within us. Prayer is a conversational wind pattern that urges us to move with the gyres of God in the world. Constantly barraging God with our anxious pleas would be a bit like setting sail straight across the Atlantic from England to America. We might get there, but we'll get there kicking and screaming, rather than aligning the sail of our souls to the pattern of love and grace. God will not be fighting against us; rather, God will be smiling, wondering if we will turn around, join the movement of the Spirit, and be carried along with the wind at our backs.

God is, hereby, an eternal conversation—an eternal prayer—who is happening all around us. This book names the movements and patterns that encourage us to listen more carefully, so that we grow to move with God. It also names environments and circumstances that can make it difficult to hear what *God is saying to God* in us. People, places, and things want us to think we can move in whatever direction pleases us. If you are satisfied with your spiritual life, satisfied moving by your own compass and patterns, this book is not for you. However, if you hunger for righteousness and want to move with God about the world, enjoying peace even amidst the storms of life, then keep reading. Being satisfied with wherever we are spiritually leads to a righteousness that separates us from others. When we hunger for God, desiring more and more to be with Christ, righteousness becomes, as we find in both the Old and New Testaments, a pattern of life oriented to God in our relationships with others, the land, and everything in between. We'll talk more about this later. Suffice it to say, the Christian life is one patterned by liturgical movements that align our sails to the way of incarnate love.

In some sense this book is a call to action. It is a call to recognize the all-encompassing nature of following Christ in this world and seeking the face of Christ in all people, in all places, in all things. Nevertheless, this book is descriptive and not proscriptive. This is deliberate. The movement of God in our midst is to be named, attended with devotion, and continuously contemplated if we are to understand what it means to be human. This means that you and I have to attend to the movement of God where we make our lives in the world. I can't tell you how to do this, per se, for the people and places where you live are different from my own, and while love always has the same form—Christ—being attentive to Christ in others is particular to how God becomes manifest wherever we are. It is about engaging each person where they are and who they are in Christ. This cannot be objectified. Therefore, this book has more to do with gyres and wind currents than it does masts and sails. Those you will need to craft where you are. My prayer for you as you read this book is that you will increase in your awareness of and attention to this conversation, this movement of God in our midst.

William Daniel
The Abbey of the Genesee
The Feast of St. Albert the Great, 2018

Acknowledgments

This book is born out of many conversations and experiences growing up in a Christian home, among good friends, and an unbelievably supportive wife and children: Amanda, Wyles, and Aydah. My family endures much just living with me, not to mention my stealing away to research and write. I love you dearly. We all come from somewhere, and I come from the Church of the Nazarene in Midland Valley, South Carolina. Growing up in the holiness tradition taught me many things. More than anything it taught me a deep longing for Christ, and to attend to Christ with all my heart, soul, mind, and strength. I am grateful to everyone along the way who has borne witness to the life of grace. I am especially thankful for all who encouraged me as I embarked on the Canterbury Trail, and for those in St. John's, Tampa, who supported me in becoming an Episcopal priest. It is really you who are to blame for what follows.

For my love of theology and my constant searching for God, I blame Steven Hoskins, who I hope will forgive me for my many mishaps and shortcomings. Henry Spaulding is accountable for making me a Platonist, though it could be worse. Stanley Hauerwas is responsible for my continued drive for theology. Only he can call you a "shit" and make you want to know more. I give thanks to God for Susan Keefe, who showed me what real faith looks like. May she rest peacefully as she continues her journey toward Christ. For Janet and Bob Gilliam, to whom this book is dedicated, I really don't have words to express my gratitude. You have cared for our family beyond measure, and I see Christ in you.

I am especially grateful to the numerous persons who bothered to think and speak Christ with me throughout the past two decades—even those who spoke hate. I have seen Christ in each encounter and through every conversation. The list is too long to include everyone, and I am sure to leave someone out, but know that I am grateful for you. A special thanks to my parents Bill and Fay Daniel, David Winchester, Dale Benson, Schuy Weishaar, Carson Walden, all the families at Church of the Good Shepherd in Raleigh, David Cawthorn, Frank Valdez, Hugh Cruse, Elizabeth Bass, Randy Hehr, Mark Wastler, John Milbank, Catherine Pickstock, D. Stephen Long, James K. A. Smith; to everyone at Nashotah House: Jason and Sharon Murbarger, Charleston and Malacy Wilson, Joseph Kucharski, Tom Holtzen, Garwood Anderson, Stephen Peay; for everyone at the Abbey of the Genesee: Brother Christian, Father Isaac Slater, Mike Sauter; to Johnnie Ross, and to the people of Saint Michael's Church, Geneseo, New York, and most especially to my bishop, the Rt. Rev. Prince G. Singh, whose love and encouragement knows no bounds. Last, but not least, I am especially grateful to Kyle David Benett and Harris Bechtol—you're both wrong about most things, and you need more Maximus Confessor in your life, but I love you as brothers and our conversations mean the world.

What Is Liturgy?

If then there is any encouragement in Christ, any consolation from love, any sharing in the Spirit, any compassion and sympathy, make my joy complete: be of the same mind, having the same love, being in full accord and of one mind. Do nothing from selfish ambition or conceit, but in humility regard others as better than yourselves. Let each of you look not to your own interests, but to the interests of others. Let the same mind be in you that was in Christ Jesus, who, though he was in the form of God, did not regard equality with God as something to be exploited, but emptied himself, taking the form of a slave, being born in human likeness. And being found in human form, he humbled himself and became obedient to the point of death—even death on a cross. Therefore God also highly exalted him and gave him the name that is above every name, so that at the name of Jesus every knee should bend, in heaven and on earth and under the earth, and every tongue should confess that Jesus Christ is Lord, to the glory of God the Father. Therefore, my beloved, just as you have always obeyed me, not only in my presence, but much more now in my absence, work out your own salvation with fear and trembling; for it is God who is at work in you, enabling you both to will and to work for his good pleasure.

—Philippians 2:1-13

In *The Mother Tongue,* Bill Bryson describes a Japanese driver's manual that has been translated into English for expatriates who need to take the driving test in Japan. In the section discussing the right of way for pedestrians, it reads this way: "When a passenger of the foot heave in sight, tootle the horn, trumpet at him melodiously at first, but if he still obstacles your passage, tootle him with vigor. . . ."[1] I don't know about you, but I've never heard anyone "trumpet at me melodiously," although I have had people "tootle me with vigor." There are obvious flaws in the translation, and the manual has clearly been translated by someone for whom English is not their native tongue.[2]

> Jesus does not take us to the Father by going on that journey as our representative and carrying us along with him by throwing out sacramental lifelines. Jesus goes to the Father in our experience of him as victim, which is our experience of ourselves as forgiven and cut loose from our self-made world. —Sebastian Moore

This is a primary example of why Alasdair MacIntyre says that "a language cannot be translated; it can only be learned." Language is cultural; it is not a strand of words thrown together. It is not separable from the person speaking or listening, nor is it separable from the places where we speak and listen. It is interwoven with our gestures and movements, our habits and practices, which are always part of a community of interpretation. In a word, language is attached, and it is attached to the people who use it, the places where it is used, and the things involved in our speaking. It attaches us to the people, places, and things with whom we interact on a daily basis. This is why a language can only be learned. When we translate, too much is lost.

This book is about the untranslatability of language. More than this, it is about the rootedness of Christian speech in a habit of liturgy. Liturgy, however, is not universal. Many churches worship differently,

---

1. Bill Bryson, *The Mother Tongue* (New York: HarperCollins Publishing, 1990), 11.
2. Ibid.

which means parishioners in one church will speak and think differently about the life of faith, and even about God, whether or not they are part of the same denomination. Not all Episcopalians, for instance, speak the same language because not all Episcopalians worship in the same manner—even churches that use the same Book of Common Prayer.

In what follows, we will unpack this dynamic relationship between thought, word, and deed as it relates to the people, places, and things involved in the liturgical life of a community. But first, we need to *unlearn* something about "liturgy." For starters, liturgy is not the "work of the people." The word liturgy comes from the Greek *leitourgia*. This is usually parsed out in the following manner: *leito = people*; *ourgia = work*. Hence, "the work of the people." This is what is commonly called a "word-for-word" translation. It's similar to translating *compromiso* in Spanish to "compromise" in English. The words look the same, they even sound the same, but whereas English usage tends to imply that two parties have made concessions and have arrived at a synthesized conclusion, or one party has given in to another's desire, Spanish usage falls more in line with the historic meaning of the word: with promise, or commitment. (Interestingly, if you insert "compromise" into Google Translate and ask for the Spanish equivalent you get *compromiso*. However, if you reverse this and enter *compromiso* to get the English translation you receive "commitment," as in "I commit myself.") In the late nineteenth century, *leitourgia* was similarly misunderstood. With this misunderstanding the worship of the church is reduced to an all too human action.

Now, don't get me wrong. We do participate in worship; however, this translation fails to call our attention to worship as an involvement in the self-offering of Christ—suddenly it's *my* offering. If we translate *leitourgia* according to its use in the New Testament, the Septuagint, as well as how it is employed well into the Middle Ages, we get something like this: *the work of one for the sake of many.*[3] Now we have a very different understanding of worship. As *the work of one for the sake of*

---

3. For a complete genealogy of the term *leitourgia* and the importance of its translation, see William Daniel, *Christ the Liturgy* (New York: Angelico Press, Ltd., 2019), ch. 1.

many, liturgy calls our attention to what God is doing in worship. We are hereby involved in an action that transcends *our* ability to act, yet in no way reduces us to passive spectators.

In his letter to the Philippians, Paul speaks of this regarding Epaphroditus's liturgy: "Still, I think it necessary to send to you Epaphroditus—my brother and co-worker and fellow soldier, your messenger and liturgist to my need. . . ."[4] Epaphroditus's liturgy is for Paul's sake. Epaphroditus does act, but his actions benefit Paul. The emphasis for Paul, however, comes in verse 30: "because [Epaphroditus] came close to death *for the work of Christ*, risking his life to make up for those *liturgies* that you could not give me." For Paul, liturgy is the work of Christ done by one person for the benefit of others. Epaphroditus and Paul are hereby "co-workers" in the work of Christ: Christ's liturgy. In other words, when I serve others, I do so as a participant in the work of Christ. I become a co-worker—a co-liturgist with Christ. I am enjoined to the self-sacrifice of Christ because I act—not in a way that benefits me but instead inhabits the offering of Christ, whose sacrifice is always an offering to the Father, even though it is for the life of the world.[5]

This understanding of liturgy focuses our attention solely on God, just as Jesus's self-offering is always in obedience to the Father. God the Son—Jesus of Nazareth—is the only person who can make an offering to God the Father. Jesus is uniquely positioned, as Second Person of the Trinity, to give to God. Why? Because only God can make an offering to God. What may at first seem contradictory or to belittle what we do week after week when we gather for worship is perhaps the single most reassuring claim we can make about the liturgy of the church. As Rowan Williams has pointed out in *Tokens of Trust*, the most reassuring thing we Christians know about God is that God doesn't need us.[6] If this were not true—if we could make an offering to God on our own—this would mean that God needs something from us that God doesn't have. If there is something that God lacks, then the triune God revealed in

---

4. Phil. 2:25.
5. John 6:51.
6. Rowan Williams, *Tokens of Trust* (Louisville: John Knox Press, 2007), 3-30.

Jesus couldn't possibly be God. What it means for God to be God is for the Trinity to be full and complete in their Oneness. *God is completely God without us.* And, paradoxically, this is why we can trust God. The God revealed in Jesus of Nazareth does not need our worship. Jesus is the only offering that God "needs," which is to say that God needs only God to be God. Therefore, what God does—because God needs nothing from us—is always for our benefit because, unlike us, God has no ulterior motive. God only ever acts according to God's nature as absolute love, without a need to be loved by what is not God. God doesn't even need us to love God in return. God is love, which means there is nothing missing in the life of God. Nothing could be more reassuring, knowing that God has created us for our enjoyment of God's very life.

Recognizing that Jesus is the One who can offer himself to the Father does not, however, reduce what we offer in worship. On the contrary, in Christ we now have something to offer; we are enabled to worship. In Christ we are blessed; by Christ we are chosen; through Christ we are adopted; all to the praise of his glory.[7] "All things," reminds the Chronicler, "come from you, [O Lord,] and of your own have we given you."[8]

What does all this mean? It means that liturgy is a gift. It means Jesus himself is liturgy. What we do when we gather for worship is participate in this particular and peculiar divine action that is always happening in the very life of the triune God. Our worship is enjoined to a worship that is always taking place.[9] As we proclaim in our Eucharistic prayers, we join "our voices with Angels and Archangels and with all the company of heaven, who for ever sing this hymn to proclaim the glory of your Name."[10]

Commenting on the liturgy, St. Irenaeus (d. 202) writes,

We offer to [God] his own, announcing consistently the fellowship and union of the flesh and Spirit. For as the bread, which is produced from the earth, when it receives the invocation of God, is no longer common bread, but the Eucharist . . . so also our bodies,

---

7. Eph. 1:3-6.
8. 1 Chron. 29:14.
9. Rev. 4.
10. BCP, 362, 367.

when they receive the Eucharist, are no longer corruptible, having the hope of the resurrection to eternity. Now we make offering to him, not as though he stood in need of it, but rendering thanks for his gift, and thus sanctifying what has been created. . . .[11]

Irenaeus carries forward Paul's theology of liturgy, reminding us that when we worship we are gathering together the gifts of God, offering to God what God first gave to us, and in this way are we transformed by grace and united with Christ in his singular offering to the Father. We gather, then, to give thanks for this union we have received in Christ, made one with his offering, in, by, and through which we become, as St. Chrysostom says, "little Christs." Our participation in Christ's offering is how we are transformed into Christ. We *become* Christ in worship—the image in which we are created, which is why Paul tells the Ephesians that, "There is one body and one Spirit . . . one Lord, one faith, one baptism, one God and Father of all, who is above all and through all and in all."[12] Our body is Christ's; our faith is Christ's; our baptism is Christ's; our Father is Christ's. This is what Paul means when he says that "[to] live is Christ. . . ."[13] I don't know about you, but this makes me want to go to church!

Even though we are created, even though we are dust and to dust we shall return,[14] Christ is immortal, and in Christ we have life, and life abundant. Not only does this take the pressure off us to get everything right, it also gives us good work to do, which is why we pray at the close of our celebrations of Holy Eucharist, "And now, Father, send us out to do the work you have given us to do. . . ."[15] It's the same reason we commit ourselves in the Baptismal Covenant, not simply to do this work, but to do so *with God's help.* Because Christ is Liturgy, we know that the work we do is a work that Christ is doing in us.[16] Because Christ is

---

11. Irenaeus, "Against Heresies," in *Ante-Nicene Fathers: The Writings of the Fathers down to A.D. 325*, ed. Alexander Roberts, James Donaldson, and A. Cleveland Coxe (Peabody: Hendrickson Publishers, 1994), IV.xviii.5-6.
12. Eph. 4:4-6; BCP, 299.
13. Phil. 1:21.
14. Psalm 103:14; BCP, 265.
15. BCP, 366.
16. 1 John 4:4.

liturgy, we can do all things through him who is our strength.[17] Because Christ is liturgy, we have received life in the Spirit.[18] Because Christ is liturgy, life is at work in us.[19]

In the following chapters, I offer an account of what it means for us to inhabit and to be inhabited by the life of liturgy that is Christ—what it means to be inhabited grace. I offer a way to (1) rethink what we do when we pray and how when we pray we do not so much call on God for help but enjoin ourselves to a conversation—the eternal conversation within the triune God. I discuss (2) how we learn to think about God through certain habits and practices, and how even our posture affects our perception of who God is and what it means to follow Christ. We will also discuss the call of liturgy on our lives (3) to be reconciled with our neighbors, and to be reconciled with all of creation. We will delve into the mystery of (4) Holy Eucharist and how feasting on Christ shapes our understanding of the body—both our individual bodies and the corporate body, the church. At the close, I offer a way to (5) reflect on your rule of life. We all have a rule of life. More often than not, however, we acquire this rule by accident, rather than through thoughtful discernment. I offer tools for forming a deliberate rule of life that will help ground you in the transcendent life of liturgy. (6) I share some stories of personal habits and practices that help me pattern my everyday life on the movements of Christ as I strive to inhabit the way of incarnate love. More importantly, it is my hope that after reading this book you will have a renewed sense of the great gift we have in the liturgy of the church and how it far surpasses our understanding, and the numerous ways our liturgy calls us to act—to work the works of Christ.[20] In other words, it is my hope that you will come to know in your body the work that Christ has begun in you and obtain new tools for inhabiting this work more deeply.

God's speed in your journey.

---

17. Phil. 4:13.
18. Rom. 8:11.
19. 2 Cor. 4:12.
20. John 6:28.

PART 1

Spoken into Being

"When you pray . . ."

When you are praying, do not heap up empty phrases as the Gentiles do; for they think that they will be heard because of their many words. Do not be like them, for your Father knows what you need before you ask him. Pray then in this way: Our Father in heaven, hallowed be your name. Your kingdom come. Your will be done, on earth as it is in heaven. Give us this day our daily bread. And forgive us our debts, as we also have forgiven our debtors. And do not bring us to the time of trial, but rescue us from the evil one. For if you forgive others their trespasses, your heavenly Father will also forgive you; but if you do not forgive others, neither will your Father forgive your trespasses. And whenever you fast, do not look dismal, like the hypocrites, for they disfigure their faces so as to show others that they are fasting. Truly I tell you, they have received their reward. But when you fast, put oil on your head and wash your face, so that your fasting may be seen not by others but by your Father who is in secret; and your Father who sees in secret will reward you.

Matthew 6:7-18

CHAPTER 1

Surprised by Prayer

Like is known only by like. Only he who abides in love can recognize love, and in the same way his love is to be known.

Søren Kierkegaard

Our children were all going trick-or-treating together for Halloween, so Amanda and I invited everyone over to our house for a quick dinner before going out. Everyone was dressed in their costumes, and as it so often happens around holiday festivities the children were excited and the parents were tired and cranky. To make things simple, we ordered pizza and had it delivered. After the pizza arrived we got our children settled at the table and invited everyone to join us in prayer.

Praying can seem awkward when you're around friends who may or may not go to church or may or may not want anything to do with God, but in our house when you eat you pray. It has always been our custom to do so regardless of the gathering or wherever we find ourselves. If I know that our guests are predominantly nonreligious I usually say something to the effect of, "You're in the priest's home, so we're going to pray before we eat. I don't want any of you to choke." So I offered a brief prayer, mindful that children had pizza in front of their faces and knowing that God is quick to listen, and as soon as we said, "Amen," one of the young boys, whose family happened to attend another Episcopal church down the road, blurted out, "Well that's the first time we've done that in about two years!" His mother, who was standing next to me, the priest, turned about three shades of red while the rest of us, including the father, attempted to restrain our laughter, though with little success.

It was quite a moment, as you can imagine. But it was understandable, because in most situations, especially as children, the reactions we have reflect our habits of life—or the habits of our parents, in this case. Our lives are a sort of mirror that reveals to others who we really are by the image we reflect through our speech and action, especially when we shout it loudly for all to hear. The child's reaction to praying before a meal revealed that for him prayer is out of the ordinary, which means that, whether or not his family prays over meals at Thanksgiving, Christmas, or Easter, it's not enough for it to feel normal.

It's not enough for prayer to happen every once in a while. It's not enough for us to pray on occasion. As Paul writes in his letter to the Thessalonians, we are to "pray without ceasing."[1] We are to be in constant conversation with God, so much so that it should strike us as awkward when we don't pray over a meal, before bed, when we wake up, throughout the day, for our friends, neighbors, and enemies. When our knee-jerk reaction to prayer is surprise, we have a problem. In every encounter, in every setting, we should rather be surprised if these do not begin with some petition or thanksgiving.

When our son was born, Amanda and I began praying the Lord's Prayer each night before bed. We wanted to make sure our children grew up in a house of prayer and would always know that prayer is normal and bookends our days. We've never neglected this habit. On the few occasions that Amanda and I have been exhausted, or in haste to get our children to bed, and we forgot to pray, our kids reminded us. Our son and daughter are now teenagers, and we've begun staying up later than we once did. However, our son is an old soul, and his bedtime

---

1. 1 Thess. 5:17.

comes earlier than for the rest of us. So nearly every night, he gets his shower, wanders downstairs, and interrupts whatever we're doing and says, "Can we pray?"

Amanda and I do not claim to be great parents. I'm pretty sure I've seriously damaged my children with my overuse of sarcasm. Nevertheless, we know that we've done at least one thing right, and that is praying daily with our children. I was a pretty good kid growing up, but I never once said to my parents before going to bed, "Can we pray?" My sixteen-year-old son reminds us to pray at night, not because Amanda and I have done something right; rather, this is what praying the Lord's Prayer for sixteen years has done to him. Praying the Lord's Prayer in our home has had an interesting effect on our life together as a family. It's surprising in our home not when we pray but when we fail to pray. This is how it should be—we should be shocked when prayer doesn't happen.

CHAPTER 2

Mirror, Mirror

Knowledge of God is not a subject's conceptual grasp of an object, it is a sharing what God is—more boldly, you might say, sharing God's "experience."

Rowan Williams

The way of prayer is a life continually disciplined by words that are not our own, for the benefit of people who are not "me," always and only to the praise of Christ's glory.[2] In her children's book *No Mirrors in My Nana's House*, author Ysaye M. Barnwell tells the story of a little girl growing up in the home of her grandmother. The story is set to music and wonderfully illustrated, and we learn of a young woman growing up in what appears to be poverty but never once feeling impoverished, because there were no mirrors in her Nana's house "and the beauty of everything was in her eyes."[3]

I never knew that my skin was too black. / I never knew that my nose was too flat. / I never knew that my clothes didn't fit. / I never

---

2. Eph. 1:12.
3. Ysaye M. Barnwell, *No Mirrors in My Nana's House* (Orlando: Harcourt Brace & Co., 1998).

knew there were things that I'd missed, / cause the beauty in everything was in her eyes.[4]

The little girl never sees herself except as one seen by her grandmother. To her grandmother she is perfectly black; she has a perfect
nose; her clothes fit just right; and everything needful is in abundance.

The world outside was a magical place. / I only knew love. / I never
knew hate, / and the beauty in everything was in her eyes.[5]

The gaze of her grandmother, whose invitation to see was, "Chil' look
deep into my eyes . . . ,"[6] is the lens through which the young girl sees
everything, even herself. It is the vision of one who knows only as they
are known.

This is the vision that Paul writes about in his first letter to the
Corinthians. "For now we see in a mirror, dimly, but then we will see
face to face. Now I know only in part; then I will know fully, even as I
have been fully known."[7] Paul is referring here to the wisdom available
to us as humans, which is the philosopher's charge to "know yourself."
As the early fathers of the church taught, we *can* know God, but only
through God's energies—only through the numerous ways God is made
manifest in creation. We know God supremely through the revelation of
Christ, but this knowledge is limited by our proximity to Christ.[8] Even
then we will never grasp the *essence* of God; we can only hope to know
God through God's activities and the revelation of Christ. What we are
most capable of knowing, however, is our creatureliness—our nature as
creatures intimately related to a Creator-God. When we truly know ourselves we come to know God in part. This is what Paul is suggesting,
which is why he likens it to seeing through a mirror darkly.

All of us have looked into a mirror. Few of us may have seen an
ancient mirror, a mirror like the one Paul would have seen or used. In

---

4. Ibid.
5. Ibid.
6. Ibid.
7. 1 Cor. 13:12.
8. Eph. 2.

first-century Palestine, the only mirrors available would have been ones hammered out in metal. There were no glass mirrors at the time. They saw an image reflected to them through the metal, including any number of blemishes. Even looking into a pool of water may have been clearer. Like the young girl in the storybook, people living in antiquity would have relied on friends and family to tell them whether they were beautiful or ugly, or whether they had something stuck in their teeth. They saw as they were seen. Even when glass was eventually used to make mirrors there remained blemishes and bubbles that prevented the viewer from seeing his or her image clearly.

There is a seismic shift, however, in the fourteenth century. Venetian glassmakers perfected a technique that, while initially involving a bevel in the glass, eliminated the blemishes and bubbles from mirrors.[9] At first these were small handheld mirrors; however, as the technology improved the size increased. Finally a person could look into a mirror and see their image perfectly reflected. No longer do we see with Paul in a mirror darkly; we now see clearly the image in which we are created—the image of God.

It should come as no surprise that this is when self-portraits came to dominate the world of art. Even many, if not most, of the paintings created during the Renaissance describe a variety of biblical narratives using the face of the artist's patron as the face of a saint or angel. One thinks of the Medici family in this regard. A person's attention is more and more on their own face and with whom their face is associated. There is a marvelous example in the Sistine Chapel where Michelangelo uses the face of a cardinal as the head of a demon. Cardinal Biago was tattling to the pope about the excessive nudity displayed in Michelangelo's painting, so he painted the prude cardinal's face on the naked demon, Minos, who watches over the gates of hell. (One should never tattle on a capable painter.)

Needless to say, the natural result of the clear, stainless mirror, which made it possible for humans to see their image perfectly reflected, led to

9. For a history of the mirror and how it developed over time, see Sabine Melchior-Bonnet, *The Mirror: A History* (New York: Routledge, 2001).

a heightened emphasis on the self. Humanism and the mirror go hand in hand. Just try looking into a mirror and not thinking about yourself, your appearance, how beautiful or handsome you are, or about the blemishes on your face, perhaps the flatness of your nose, or that you have too much or too little pigmentation. It's unavoidable. Except, perhaps, if we get rid of all the mirrors.

Gregory of Nyssa, one of the great Cappadocian fathers of the church who paved the way for our firm belief in the Trinity, has an alternative vision of what a mirror is. Gregory describes *us*, namely our souls, as mirrors. Just as a mirror takes on the image of whatever is placed in front of it, says Gregory, so we take on the image we place before ourselves. "If you put gold in front of a mirror," he writes, "the mirror takes on the appearance of the gold and because of the reflection it shines with the same gleam as the real substance."[10] Gregory goes on to say that "if it catches the reflection of something loathsome, it imitates this ugliness by means of a likeness, as for example a toad, a millipede, or anything else that is disgusting to look at."[11]

I may not look like a toad or a millipede if I stand in front of them, though I suppose I might by association, but I have noticed this mirror effect of other things, even certain dramas, on my disposition. The Netflix series *House of Cards* is one example. As the series progressed it became darker and darker. With each episode I noticed my posture shifting. I found myself at the end of each episode a little more slumped over than when I first turned it on. It's a well-produced show, which is why I kept watching. Increasingly, however, I found myself wearing the violence of the characters. I grew sadder and sadder as the characters chose courses of action that mingled their lives with hate. (Amanda stopped watching the show altogether; she's holier than I am.) But I became intrigued by the effect it was having on me. This is what Gregory is suggesting in his *Commentary on the Song of Songs*. Whatever we place ourselves in front of will come to inhabit us as a disposition. If I put before myself things that elicit hate and violence, I will slowly take on hate and violence as a disposition.

10. Gregory of Nyssa, *Commentary on the Song of Songs,* Sermon II.
11. Ibid.

To clarify, this may or may not mean that I become violent or hateful. There are mixed results from studies done on those who, for instance, play violent video games or watch violent movies. Most studies seem to suggest that doing so does *not* make a person more violent. What they do show, however, is that these persons often become apathetic to violence. In other words, I may not become actively violent or hateful, but I may become passively violent and hateful, ignoring the suffering of others or simply ignoring others altogether. As a mirror, I take on the sensibilities of that to which I am most attentive. I become a spectator to violence, a spectator to the suffering of others. We take on the disposition of the people, places, and things that know us, whatever it is we place in front of us—whatever we place ourselves in front of.

We are all known by particular people, places, and things. We don't generally think in these terms, or at least not about these being bearers of self-knowledge. We think of ourselves as autonomous, self-knowing, even self-aware in our autonomy. The only problem with this notion is that none of us live in a vacuum. We were not dropped here from the sky. We all came from somewhere; we all have histories, families, and hopefully friends, all of which inform who we are. The difficulty is that objects like mirrors deceive us into believing that we are the fairest of them all. They turn us inward in negative ways that make us think we are individuals separable from others. We come to believe that we can write our own stories and choose our own histories. We choose our destinies instead of receiving ourselves as destined from God.

So how do we remedy this? How do we come to recognize that our lives are not our own,[12] that we did not choose God but God in Christ chose us?[13] If Paul and Gregory are right, and if the wisdom of a child really is the way,[14] then it begins by placing before the mirror of our souls people, places, and things that draw out from us the truth of our nature hidden in Christ. It begins by removing from our lives anything that turns us back on ourselves as woefully independent.

---

12. 1 Cor. 6:19.
13. John 15:16.
14. Isa. 11.

We take on the *likeness*, says Gregory, of whatever we place before the mirror of our souls. Early theologians use this word *likeness* to refer to our thoughts, words, and deeds. We are created in the *image* of God, they tell us, but *likeness* to Christ in what we think, say, and do is how we become aware of our true nature as *imago Dei*—the image of God. God creates us in his image and for his purposes but God does not force the way of love upon us. It is always and forever a gift we are to receive with humility. The way we receive this gift is through what Maximus Confessor calls *volitive participation*.

Volitive participation is not to be mistaken for voluntarism. Voluntary association as an individual decision is one of the great sins of the modern church. *Volitive* is best understood as a *willful willing*—what is not *my* will. Volunteering is often associated with my decision to do something I do not have to do, as in spending the afternoon volunteering at the soup kitchen. Volitive participation, on the other hand, sounds like this: "Father, if you are willing, remove this cup from me; yet, not my will but yours be done."[15] Volitive participation is a prayerful disposition that names our frailty and inability to inhabit the will of God and yet give ourselves to being inhabited by the will of the Father. We say, "I will, *with God's help*," in our Baptismal Covenant. I do not choose to follow Jesus; I embrace my chosen-ness and relinquish my own will, which may involve helping at the soup kitchen. The difference between the two is that a volunteer is someone who acts for a temporary period of time for a purpose that may or may not be of self-interest.

A *volitive participant*, however, is one whose very life is assimilated to the form of Christ, always acting according to the will of the Father, and for the benefit of others. Volitive participation sounds like, "Our Father . . . thy will be done. . . ."

So what does volitive participation look like? In other words, what is this way of soulful mirroring?

---

15. Luke 22:42.

CHAPTER 3

The Resistless Energy of Love

God is beyond in the midst of our life.

Dietrich Bonhoeffer

A t Nashotah House, where I was a seminarian, a prayer is offered every day during Evensong or at Matins on Thursdays (as it has been for decades). It's a prayer I continue to pray even though my year of Anglican studies at Nashotah was years ago. I found myself swept up by this prayer each and every day. Certain prayers do this to us. They call us beyond ourselves but in a way that forces us to deal with ourselves all at the same time, mindful of those around us and attentive to our heavenly destiny.

The portion of the prayer that has followed me more than any other is this:

Bless all who may be trained here; take from them all pride, vanity, and self-conceit, and give them true humility and self-abasement . . . that they may speak with that resistless energy of love, which shall melt the hearts of sinners to the love of thee. . . .

A Prayer for Nashotah House

Bless, O Lord, this house, set apart to the glory of your great name and the benefit of your holy church; and grant that your Name may be worshipped here in truth and purity to all generations. Give your grace and wisdom to all the authorities, that they may exercise holy discipline, and be themselves patterns of holiness, simplicity, and self-denial. Bless all who may be trained here; take from them all pride, vanity, and self-conceit, and give them true humility and self-abasement. Enlighten their minds, subdue their wills, purify their hearts, and so penetrate them with your Spirit and fill them with your love, that they may go forth animated with earnest zeal for your glory; and may your ever living Word so dwell within their hearts, that they may speak with that *resistless energy of love* which shall melt the hearts of sinners to the love of you. Open, O Lord, the hearts and hands of your people, that they may be ready to give and glad to distribute to our necessities. Bless the founders and benefactors of this house and recompense them with the riches of your everlasting kingdom, for Jesus's sake. Amen.[16]

Jesus tells his disciples not to worry about what they are to say or how they are to say it, if they are ever brought before rulers or authorities.[17] We are not to be defensively predisposed; rather, if we live a life of humility, and our words speak the truth in love, then as the hymnist writes, the God who has been "our help in ages past" will be our sure defense.[18] Defensiveness has only the effect of hardening the hearts of our enemies. Humility, however, disarms, and silencing our speech makes room for love to do its work. The other person's anger exposes

---

16. Nashotah House Theological Seminary, Nashotah, Wisconsin, 1842. Emphasis added.

17. Luke 12.

18. Isaac Watts, "O God, Our Help in Ages Past," in *The Hymnal, 1982* (New York: Church Hymnal, 1985), 680.

itself in the space of quiet humility. Sometimes speaking the truth in love is best done with silence. Humility "melts the hearts of sinners."

A few years ago, the tragic death of three college students involved in a murder-suicide wracked our small village. The family of the assailant had been deeply embedded in the community as far back as anyone could remember, and the other two were well connected and well loved on campus and about the town. It was a crime of passion. A young man was distraught over his ex-girlfriend becoming involved with another young man. It's a common story. In the wake of their deaths we held a vigil in our church for all three who had died, not just the two that were killed.

In my homily, I mentioned having received a phone call from an anonymous woman. She called after hours and left a message for me, informing me that I should be ashamed of myself for holding a service in remembrance of all three young people instead of just the two who had been murdered. She said that by praying for the forgiveness of the killer I was betraying God. Growing up in the American South, and having lived in the North, I am all too aware that we Americans tend to define ourselves by opposition. It's a very *Protest*ant thing to do, and this has been the most difficult aspect of our Puritan heritage to shake. The woman, safe in her anonymity, would have had me condemn the young man for his crime and remember to God only those who had been murdered. This understanding of prayer is a far cry from Jesus's cry from the cross, "Father, forgive them, for they know not what they do."[19] And if there was anything the young man didn't know, it was what he was doing. No one who takes the life of another or their own life can possibly know what they are doing.

Our prayer is always to be a prayer of forgiveness. Our prayer is always for the sake of those who have wronged us *and* those whom we have wronged. When we slip into a "holier than thou" posture of prayer our words become contemptible. They are like the prayer of the Pharisee in the Temple who cries out to God, "God, I thank you that I am not like

---

19. Luke 23:34.

other people: thieves, rogues, adulterers, or even like this tax collector."[20]
And while we think this is a far cry from our own imaginations, how
many of us have said, "I'm glad that's not *my* child." "I'm glad *my* spouse
doesn't act like that." "I'm glad *my* parents taught me better."

Our words are all too often defensive. We are so ready to defend
our own practices, our own children, our own way of life that we
refuse to acknowledge our complicity—we refuse to acknowledge that
we are sinners.

"My anonymous caller is right about one thing," I said as I scanned
the room. "[Jonathan]" (and I use a pseudonym) "does not deserve forgiveness." After a brief pause to let everyone's anxiety stir, I continued
with greater emphasis. "And neither do any of us."

To speak with the *resistless energy of love* requires that we place
before the mirror of our souls the desire of God and the way of radical
forgiveness. All too often we place our own and often petty concerns
before the mirror of our souls, which elicits a kind of spiritual schizo-
phrenia, an inner dialogue of self-interests, fearful of everyone but ourselves. This is why intercession is the primary form of prayer. If I am not
first and foremost concerned with the needs and concerns of others in
prayer, what I want will always cloud my judgment and my speech. I will
not speak with resistless love because my concerns will only be *my* concerns. There is nothing irresistible about self-centeredness.

This is why silence is so important, not simply as a daily habit but
in prayer and conversation. Stephen Covey famously said, "Most people
listen not with the intent to understand but with the intent to reply."[21]
We listen defensively. Vehicles of "conversation" (and I use this term
loosely) such as Facebook and Twitter are symptomatic of our defensive tendencies—our desire to avoid silence, serving only to deafen our
hearts to others. Defensive listening comes from a heart that is either
not disciplined by prayer or a heart disciplined by prayers that are self-
justifying rather than humbly attentive. When my prayers have me at

---

20. Luke 18:11.
21. Stephen Covey, *The 7 Habits of Highly Effective People* (New York: Simon and
Schuster, 2004), 251.

the center, my desire to pontificate supersedes my ability to listen with understanding. Rather than opening myself to be seen and known by others, and thereby reflecting the humility of Christ, I reject receiving myself from others, locating my identity and personhood in my autonomous self. "The practice of silence," however, "is an agent of healing in a world of harmful words and wordiness."[22]

Our manner of speaking hereby makes manifest the truth of our prayers. It's hard to hate someone whom we bring before God in prayer. It's easier to hear the person we entrust to God's love and forgiveness. If I have a habit of speaking negatively about someone behind their back, telling others how they have harmed me and wronged me, or of my general dislike for them, the only thing this reveals is my own habit of prayer, or lack thereof. What I say about anyone, regardless of its truth, says more about me than it does about the other person. It reveals my prayerful disposition, which is either formed by intercessions and concerns for another's well-being or my own self-interests. To speak with *that resistless energy of love* is contingent upon a heart humbly disposed for the good of others, even those we count as enemies.

---

22. Kyle David Bennett, *Practices of Love: Spiritual Disciplines for the Life of the World* (Grand Rapids: Brazos Press, 2017), 125.

CHAPTER 4

Inhabited by Prayer

The church is not a religious cult but a liturgy, embracing the entire creation of God.

Alexander Schmemann

Dietrich Bonhoeffer writes in *Life Together*:

> God's word seeks to enter in and remain with us. It strives to stir us to work and operate in us, so that we shall not get away from it the whole day long. Then it will do its work in us, often without our being conscious of it.[23]

Can we imagine prayer as something that operates in us, the word of God coming to life in our prayers, as opposed to petitions that we hope cause some stirring in God? The Old Testament tells the story of a God who is persuaded by his people, or at least is open to being persuaded. Recall in Genesis 18 that Abraham negotiates with God over Sodom and Gomorrah. Abraham reminds God that he is not one to throw the baby out with the bathwater, that God is not one to slay the righteous with the wicked. "If I can find fifty people, would you spare the city?"

---

23. Dietrich Bonhoeffer, *Life Together*, trans. John W. Doberstein (New York: Harper and Row Publishers, 1954), 83.

And God replies, "Sure." Abraham can't find fifty, so he comes back and says, "How about forty-five?" "Sure," God says again. "How about forty . . . thirty . . . twenty . . . ten . . . ?" By the time we get to the end of the encounter we have not so much found God changing his mind as we find Abraham recognizing that God does in fact know what needs to be done. Prayer, you might say, is a patient conversation with God where we learn to trust the will of God above our own desires and understanding.

To suggest that prayer is operative in us is to become attentive to the truth of our nature as mediated by God. As we discussed in the introduction, liturgy is our participation in an action that is not our own, even though we are involved in the act. In like manner, to pray is to be caught up in the ongoing and eternal conversation between the Father and the Son, whose Spirit incorporates us into this divine communion. This conversation began long before we entered the scene, but by the grace of God it does not continue apart from our involvement.

In The General Thanksgiving of Morning and Evening Prayer in the Book of Common Prayer, we pray that God would "give us that due sense of all thy mercies, that our hearts may be unfeignedly thankful."[24] If our hearts are to be *unfeignedly thankful* we must receive from God *merciful sensibilities*. So how does a person receive merciful sensibilities? "Blessed are the merciful," Jesus says in the Sermon on the Mount, "for they shall receive mercy."[25] Mercy-filled sensibilities occur in one whose way of life is the way of mercy—Christ.

In the Prayer of Humble Access, we pray to the God "whose property is always to have mercy. . . ."[26] It may be the most amazing prayer in the Book of Common Prayer. In it we acknowledge that apart from Christ we deserve nothing, but in Christ we receive everything, even bread from heaven. If God's property is always to have mercy, and if we really are created in the image of God, then the core of our nature as humans is mercy. In showing mercy in every aspect of our lives, with everyone we meet (even the person driving too slowly down the highway

---

24. BCP, 59.
25. Matt. 5.
26. BCP, 337.

or the one riding our bumper in town), we come to know ourselves first and foremost as we are known—by mercy. In showing mercy toward the one who has done nothing but slander us and stab us in the back, we come to know ourselves as we are known by the One who was himself slandered and stabbed in the back, even by those who were his followers. When we show mercy as Christ shows mercy, the very work of mercy comes alive in us and gives us the silent confidence to speak love to the hateful and absorb the violence of this world, so that the cycle of violence does not continue. Christ's liturgy of mercy operates in us well beyond the liturgical gathering, calling us again and again to the truth of what Maximus Confessor terms our "natural nature"—calling us to merciful sensibilities. We speak, through our prayerful participation, with the irresistible energy of love.

"You hear nothing true from my lips," says St. Augustine, "which you have not first told me."[27] What comes from our lips is always mediated through a habit of prayer. If that is true, it is evidence of Christ's prayer at work in us. If that is false, it is evidence of a self-centeredness rooted in fear. Falsehood originates with us, with our sin and neglect of the things of God. It is our succumbing to the temptations of the world because we lack the centeredness found only in a habit of prayer. When we attend to merciful sensibilities, as we pray in the General Thanksgiving, we show forth the praise of God "not only with our lips, but in our lives," and we *give up* ourselves to God's service, "walking before thee in holiness and righteousness all our days; through Jesus Christ our Lord."[28] Hatred, anger, animosity, and lack of forgiveness do not show forth the praise of God. These characteristics manifest a neglected conversation with God. Even Christ, when he teaches us to pray, says that we should pray to the Father saying, "forgive us our sins *as* we forgive those who sin against us." This is also the binding that Jesus talks about regarding the power of his followers: "Whatever you bind on earth will be bound in heaven."[29]

---

27. St. Augustine, *Confessions,* trans. Henry Chadwick (Oxford: Oxford University Press, 1991), X.ii.
28. BCP, 58-59.
29. Matt. 16.

When I forgive, I do not simply release my offender; I release myself from sin's hold over both of our lives. When I refuse to forgive, I bind myself to the sin of the other. I create a chasm between God and me, binding myself to dust and ashes. My enemy, however, may yet find reconciliation with God when I refuse to forgive. It is I who refuse to receive God's forgiveness when I decline to let go of sin's hold over me because of my neighbor's action. If I do not show mercy—if I do not forgive—I cannot expect to be shown mercy.[30] I cannot expect to be forgiven. These are not the actions of one inhabited by prayer. These are the actions of one who is still trying to control the outcome of prayer. These are the actions of one who has not yet *willingly willed* the will of God. Until I hand over control and forgive even the unforgivable, I will continue to think that I deserve God's grace and forgiveness. I will continue to think that God somehow needs me, and my arrogance will be my downfall.

This is why it is so important that most prayers in the Book of Common Prayer end with, "*through* Jesus Christ our Lord. . . ." When I recognize that nothing good I say or pray originates with me but courses through me by the grace of God, only then will my words become charged with divine, resistless energy. Only when my prayers are conditioned by the speech of Christ will I come to know who I really am. "Unless he utters himself in you, speaks his own name in the center of your soul," says Thomas Merton, "you will no more know him than a stone knows the ground upon which it rests in its inertia."[31] Likewise, says Merton, "I shall discover who I am and shall possess my true identity by losing myself in him."[32] We will continue to chase ourselves amidst identity politics until we locate our whole self, identity and all, in Christ. "This is who I am," is a far cry from Paul's declaration that, "For me to live is Christ. . . ."[33] While God reaches out to us in our particularity it is never to leave us

---

30. James 2:13.
31. Thomas Merton, *New Seeds of Contemplation* (New York: New Direction Publishing Corporation, 2007), 39.
32. Ibid.
33. Phil. 1:21.

where and how we are. Prayer calls us to a life whereby we inhabit a life that is not our own, for purposes that are not our own, in such a way that transforms our sensibilities to receive ourselves from Christ and our neighbors, even our enemies, rather than assert "my identity."

This mutual habitation, the reciprocal indwelling of Christ in the believer and the believer in Christ, is the way in which we know God at all and, consequently, know the truth of our humanity—our *natural nature*. Through sensibilities born in mercy we reveal in our thoughts, words, and deeds the character of God. By grace we speak mercy and extend mercy; in speaking mercy and performing acts of mercy we become attuned to God speaking to God, to being inhabited by grace, as the prayer of Christ's forgiveness inhabits us, enabling us to inhabit our own bodies more deeply as a people of mercy. In this way we give ourselves in volitive participation to the eternal conversation of Father, Son, and Holy Spirit. God speaks to God in us, and we participate in the mystery of the incarnation. The one thing God cannot resist in us is God; when we stop resisting the mercy of God, love and grace become operative in us, and the Incarnate Word inhabiting us becomes a resist-less energy before others.

CHAPTER 5

Prayerful Humility

If you humble yourself, God comes down from above and enters into you.

Meister Eckhart

The holy person," says Rowan Williams, "is the one 'free from passion' because he or she is the person free from having their relations totally dictated by instinct, self-defense—reactivity, as we might say these days."[34] It is hard to respond instead of react these days. As we've noted, our posture is all too often a defensive, reactive one. We lack the patience for silence as a response to our accusers, perpetrators, or even loved ones because our point of reference is not our relationship grounded in Christ, but instead "my" autonomy exercised in opposition to another's. An economics of greed, so influential through the world, has subtly reconditioned our relationships with each other, even with family. If I am going to make this much money, then you will have to make less. Such scarcity in our relationships sounds something like this: If I am going to be who I am, then you cannot be who you are. So, we make a compromise. You get to be who you are and I get to

---

34. Rowan Williams, *Holy Living: The Christian Tradition for Today* (New York: Bloomsbury Publishing Plc., 2017), 119.

be me, so long as our lives are disconnected. It's not even so generous as, "If you scratch my back, I'll scratch yours." It's more like, "If you leave my back alone, I'll leave yours alone." Conservatives and liberals hereby have clear boundaries that do not overlap, leaving us in a stalemate politically, and leaving us altogether emotionally distraught and antagonistic toward anyone who does not share the same beliefs and opinions. We are a far cry from faith seeking understanding.[35]

Our reactive and defensive language is evidence of a lack of humility. We lack a certain curiosity toward others. When I am curious about what another person thinks or believes I ask questions, in order that I might better understand. If I relate to another person on the basis of my animal instinct, fearing the other person as competition, I will react to them in self-defense and fail to hear what they have to say. If, however, my sensibilities have been re-habituated through prayer in the way of humility, even my instincts are transformed. Instead of reacting to a problem I locate in the other person, I am moved to wonder. I respond instead of react because I am curious about what Christ may be revealing in the life of the other person, but I also trust in the primacy of our relatedness in Christ, rooted in grace and not fear.

When I trust God, there is no relationship that cannot be healed. When I am the only person I trust I do not simply prohibit myself from understanding the other person, but I also keep myself from being known by God. In the process I lose all sense of who I am. It is for this reason that humility in our prayers is crucial. Humility in prayer is the prayer of the tax collector, "God, be merciful to me, a sinner!"[36] It also sounds something like this:

> O Lord, you know my heart and you know the heart of my neighbor; help me to understand myself in them, to see you in them, and to be known by you in relationship with them, so that having my

---

35. See Anselm, *Proslogium; Monologium; An Appendix in Behalf of the Fool by Gaunilon; and Cur Deus Homo*, trans. Sidney Norton Deane (Eugene: Wipf and Stock Publishers, 2003), 7. See also Ps. 14, on which Anselm bases his apology for God on the realizing that everyone has some notion of "that which nothing greater than can be thought."
36. Luke 18:13.

senses transformed by your mercy I might always show mercy, and in all things seek not so much to be understood as to understand; through Jesus Christ our Lord. *Amen.*

Imagine struggling in a relationship with someone and then praying this prayer. Humility in our relationships begins with humility in our prayers, which begins with trusting in God. If I cannot pray for God's will to be done, and for God to show me what I need to learn from my enemies, neighbors, and friends, I cannot speak and live humbly before others. I will only react to that which is not *my* instinct.

It is for this reason that the opening word in *The Rule of Saint Benedict* is *Obsculta*—"Listen."[37] Later in the prologue, describing the way of those who listen and whose eyes have been opened to the divine light, God says to this one,

> If you will have true and everlasting life, keep your tongue from evil and your lips that they speak no guile. Turn away from evil and do good; seek after peace and pursue it. And when you have done these things, my eyes shall be upon you and my ears open to your prayers; and before you call upon me, I will say to you, "Behold, here I am."[38]

Those who listen, writes Benedict, keep their tongues from evil. They are known by God and God hears them. Notice that it is not my humility that makes me audible before God; rather, humble speech is evidence of God's peace and mercy at work in me, which makes it possible for *God to hear God in me.* As Thomas Merton writes, "[God] is only known and loved by those to whom he has freely given a share in his own knowledge and love of himself."[39] This free gift of knowing God comes about through listening, a listening that involves the whole person—a union of body, mind, and soul—in attention before Christ.

37. Terrence G. Kardong, *Benedict's Rule: A Translation and Commentary* (Collegeville: The Liturgical Press, 1996), 5.
38. Benedict, *The Rule of St. Benedict*, trans. Leonard J. Doyle (Collegeville, MN: The Liturgical Press, 2001), 15 (Prologue).
39. Merton, *New Seeds of Contemplation*, 40.

When we have died with Christ, the humility of Christ that listening affords finds its home in us. "Peace here does house,"[40] writes Gerard Manley Hopkins. We become the dwelling place of God, his holy temple.[41] It is then that we see, not in a mirror darkly and not our own reflection in the mirror—we behold, at the core of our very being, "him who is my friend and not a stranger."[42] Before we see God in our bodies, as the Burial Rite of the Book of Common Prayer reminds us, we must see God in the bodies of our neighbors, in the lives of those who are not me. I will not see Christ in others if I do not entrust my enemies, friends, and neighbors to God. So long as I trust my own instincts and regard others as a threat to my identity, I do not trust God and I do not trust the energy of Christ's love to transcend what appears to separate me from my enemy, friend, or neighbor.

Remaining in my individuality I keep myself from the source of my personhood—Christ. I keep myself from my true identity as one who coheres with God in Christ. If I am only ever my own self then I will fail to become Christ. If I limit the sources of my identity to "me," I reduce myself to instinct and fail to inhabit the beloved community of God established by and sustained in Christ. This in no way reduces me to the collective; rather, through the community of Christ disciplined by prayerful humility, I learn to see myself as Christ in the other person.

We often say that we should step into the shoes of another and see the world from where they are. This is not really possible. It sounds quaint and it makes us feel like we're being empathetic, but it is at best an appreciation, which sustains our separateness. However, when I step into the shoes of another person and look not at their world but rather at myself, then I gain access to who they are, as I come more fully into light. I begin to know as I am known. Further, when I recognize that my enemy, friend, or neighbor is first and foremost a participant in the divine life, however great or little their life gives evidence of this, I can

---

40. Gerard Manley Hopkins, "Peace," in *Hopkins: Poems* (New York: Everyman's Library, 1995), 75.
41. Eph. 2.
42. BCP, 491.

begin to see who I am not simply from their vantage point but as one mutually bound to Christ.

When I see myself from where they stand, I begin to see myself as I am seen by Christ in them. I begin to see myself as one who inhabits Christ with all whom Christ inhabits, none of whom are exempt. This is to take seriously what it means to be created in the image of God. In this humble light I do not reduce the *imago Dei* to what I see in the mirror. Rather, Christ in the other becomes the mirror by which I learn to see who I am. In this manner I begin to locate my identity no longer in my own individual desires and instincts, but transcending these in the vision of myself in the Christ of my enemy, friend, and neighbor; I know myself as a cohabitant in Christ who cohabitates in us.

My relationships are hereby dictated no longer by the limits of instinct. Rather, mercy and humility, dictated by God speaking to God in me, which we now faithfully know to be prayer, reveals the truth of my identity first and foremost as known and second as knower. I am one who is known by mercy, and I now know all things in mercy. Only then do I know my enemy, friend, or neighbor, and only hereby do I know myself. "The merciful quickly grasp the truth in their neighbors," writes St. Bernard of Clairvaux in his *Steps of Humility*, "when their heart goes out to them with a love that unites them so closely that they feel the neighbors' good and ill as if it were their own."[43] We are complicit with our neighbors, both in virtue and in vice, both in suffering and in rejoicing. This complicity is known only through prayer, whereby salvation is no longer a righteousness that condemns the sin of my neighbor but a humility that owns her sin as my own. In loving her as Christ, forgiving her with the forgiveness of Christ, we are both released from sin's bondage, made free in Christ, knowing ourselves as cohabitants in Christ's mutual indwelling.

---

43. Bernard of Clairvaux, *Steps of Humility*, trans. Basil Pennington (Collegeville: Cistercian Publications, 1989), 34.

Conclusion

If it is a mark of love to be patient and kind, the one who acts contentiously or wickedly clearly makes himself a stranger to love, and the one who is a stranger to love is a stranger to God, since "God is love."

Maximus Confessor

The difficulty with prayerful humility and the form of relationship hereby called into being is that it often requires us, when we are wronged, to own our complicity in the harm done to us. This is not to suggest that we deserve to be wronged. It is, however, to suggest that when I own the good and ill of my neighbor as my own, recognizing that neither my neighbor nor I deserve grace, I can extend forgiveness as a mutual participant in forgiveness. I can extend the forgiveness that God has extended to me. When I presume that forgiveness is mine to dish out to those who are deservingly contrite, as in a judicial system, then I am like the envious vineyard worker who weighs his many hours against the brief stint of those hired toward the end of the workday.[44] I think I am more deserving because I did not commit *that* particular sin. In so doing I give sin a power it otherwise does not have, allowing our relationship to be dictated not by grace and forgiveness, but by scarcity and division. This is where pride takes over, as it did with the brother of the prodigal son who could not rejoice in his resurrected

---

44. Matt. 20.

brother. Why? The brother of the one who had squandered his wealth and returned home only saw someone who had wasted his inheritance; he could not see a brother who "came to himself,"[45] who had recognized he wasted his life yet finally came to his senses. Instead, the indignant brother saw only more waste on one who had already exploited his father. Yet the father only saw his dead son raised to newness of life. The prodigal son did not deserve forgiveness, but that wasn't the point of the parable. Rather, it highlights an understanding of forgiveness as a father anticipating his wayward son's return home, grateful that the relationship has been restored.

This understanding of grace and forgiveness is not easy. For starters, it does not allow me to exercise power over the person who has harmed me or misused what I have given. When I do withhold forgiveness it is I, not the one who wronged me, who wallows in sin. We can't get there, however, until we learn first and foremost to pray for those who have harmed us. Yet in the same manner as Abraham we hereby grow to trust the decrees of God and not our own. We come to trust the will of God and not our own. Freedom from sin, death, and anger arise when we free ourselves from sin's bondage, a bondage to which we only subject ourselves. God does not hold my sin over my head. If I am repentant no one else can hold it over me. The real harm is what I do to myself in withholding forgiveness for my neighbor.

In part 2 we will discuss how our embodied habits can incline us toward forgiveness or hardness of heart. The words that fill our prayers arise from bodily habits that condition how we perceive God and others. Building on the reality that our communication with others is grounded in our communication with God, we will see how certain gestures and postures can, in some sense, instigate or compel us to grace and forgiveness. This is not to suggest that we can somehow conjure God by moving in particular ways or saying certain prayers; rather, it is owning the reality that as the life of Christ takes on flesh in us we will speak and move in particular and peculiar ways that reveal the truth of our nature hidden in Christ.

---

45. Luke 15:17.

Discussion Questions

1. *Inhabited by Grace* suggests that we do not so much communicate with God in prayer as God communicates with God in us. How does this compare or contrast with your understanding of prayer? What concerns you about this description and what new insights have you gained regarding your life of prayer?

2. Have you ever thought about the relationship between how you pray and how you speak and relate to others? This section, part one, suggests that the two are intimately connected. Does this expose anything about what you pray for or how you speak to God in prayer?

3. This section also offers a way of self-knowing that comes from seeing ourselves through the Christ in others. Consider someone with whom you are friends or even enemies. What do you see in yourself from their shoes? How might this way of seeing increase empathy in your relationships?

PART II

Moved by the Spirit

"You are marked as Christ's own . . ."

You are the salt of the earth; but if salt has lost its taste, how can its saltiness be restored? It is no longer good for anything, but is thrown out and trampled under foot.

You are the light of the world. A city built on a hill cannot be hid. No one after lighting a lamp puts it under the bushel basket, but on the lampstand, and it gives light to all in the house. In the same way, let your light shine before others, so that they may see your good works and give glory to your Father in heaven.

Do not think that I have come to abolish the law or the prophets; I have come not to abolish but to fulfill. For truly I tell you, until heaven and earth pass away, not one letter, not one stroke of a letter, will pass from the law until all is accomplished. Therefore, whoever breaks one of the least of these commandments, and teaches others to do the same, will be called least in the kingdom of heaven; but whoever does them and teaches them will be called great in the kingdom of heaven. For I tell you, unless your righteousness exceeds that of the scribes and Pharisees, you will never enter the kingdom of heaven.

Matthew 5:13-20

CHAPTER 6

The Architecture of Prayer

Each town, each neighborhood, each building, has a particular set
of . . . patterns of events according to its prevailing culture.

Christopher Alexander

Jack Finney's short story "Where the Cluetts Are"[46] tells the story of
Sam and Ellie Cluett and the building of their new vacation home.
Sam has become a successful boat builder and his company is doing
so well that he is making more money than he and Ellie can spend. So
they decide to build their dream house. The only problem is they can't
figure out what kind of house they want to build nor where they should
build it.

After several meetings with an architect, giving him no direction
in the plans yet turning down numerous proposals along the way, Ellie
stumbles upon a set of one-hundred-year-old blueprints for a house
unlike anything they had seen or imagined. While the architect is talking
about their options, Sam and Ellie become captivated by the old plans
for this 1885 home, and Sam says to his architect, "Can you build it?"
"Well," he responds, "it would take some reconfiguring to install the

---

46. Jack Finney, "Where the Cluetts Are," in *About Time* (New York: Simon & Schuster Inc., 1986), 112-129.

plumbing and wiring, but sure, it can be done." "Let's build it," says Sam, "and I want it just like it is in the blueprints, spare no expense."

As the supplies are ordered and construction begins on the house, strange things begin to happen. For starters, the carpenters hired for the job love the work. It requires all the carpentry skills that made them want to become carpenters in the first place—skills for which a society of efficiency no longer has time or money. As the house begins to come together, small, almost unnoticeable things begin to happen. The workers building the house begin to wear nineteenth-century-style work clothes and grow facial hair of the same period—wide mustaches, sideburns, muttonchops, and more.

The most interesting transformation occurs after their home is built and Sam and Ellie begin to inhabit it. The 1885 house was intended to be a vacation home, a place the Cluetts could escape to for three or four months a year. However, after Sam and Ellie move into their new home they end up never leaving. Sam begins spending less and less time at the office, and Ellie begins doing things around the house she never dreamed of doing, even making all of her and Sam's clothing. Sam and Ellie's grammar begins to shift as well, as if they had suddenly become Victorian. The house that was intended to be a retreat from their ordinary lives had come to re-habituate their sensibilities to a new ordinary. If it weren't for the date on the calendar, walking into the Cluett home might cause one to believe that they had stepped back in time.

"Where the Cluetts Are" is not your typical time-travel fiction. Sam and Ellie do not walk through a portal or jump into a spacecraft; rather, the home they inhabit comes to inhabit them in unexpected ways. They begin to inhabit time as if standing outside of time, for it is they who are inhabited by their home—by a different sense of time. How the Cluetts come to be inhabited by that which they inhabit is analogous to the dynamic we experience when Christians gather for sacred liturgy. To inhabit the space of prayer is to become inhabited by prayerful space.

This story reveals something about prayer and our houses of prayer. It brings to mind something Christians already know about our church buildings, what we wear, our language, and even our bodies. It reminds us that these places and words, even our dress, are mutually inhabitable. A monk, for instance, wears a habit. His garment is inseparable from his habit of prayer. Prayer is not other than the clothes we wear. Habitats are places of habit—churches are houses of prayer. There is an inseparability here that often goes unnoticed, to which we now draw our attention.

Space coheres in us. As Gaston Bachelard describes in *The Poetics of Space,* the places we inhabit, especially our homes, are born in us. They are "physically inscribed in us."[47] We not only store up memories in our homes, or put holes in the drywall, as my brother and I so often did growing up, but we carry our homes with us when we leave.[48] Our homes mark us and we inhabit the world in relation to the house in which we sleep and eat, even the house(s) in which we grew up.[49] Places of prayer are likewise inscribed in us. They are habitats of memory, especially muscle memory—habit. We take on our houses of prayer as if putting on a garment or breathing air, but only to the degree that we live and move in them. To live and breathe the peace of churches, in other words, they must increasingly become our primary place, or at least one of our primary places, of habituation. Only if our churches are in some sense our spiritual oxygen tanks do they come to inhabit us and (re)orient us with them to God. The reason the Cluett home comes to dominate Ellie's and Sam's sensibilities is because the 1885 home becomes their primary residence, which they grow to inhabit more and more, preferring it to the other environments that once commanded their attention and governed their sense of time. Stepping outside of the rhythm of commerce, Sam begins to inhabit time differently. His new home is not simply a place to sleep and eat; rather, it is a world through which he and Ellie come to perceive life anew. Their life is no longer ordered by the twentieth century. Their way of being becomes nineteenth century because their home accords with the sensibilities of 1885.

---

47. Gaston Bachelard, *The Poetics of Space*, trans. Maria Jolas (Boston: Beacon Press Books, 1994), 14.
48. Colin Ellard, *Places of the Heart: The Psychogeography of Everyday Life* (New York: Bellevue Literary Press, 2015), 68.
49. Bachelard, *The Poetics of Space*, 3-37.

Architecture patterns our movements, even our grammar. We move within the boundaries of the structures in which we dwell. In *A Timeless Way of Building*, Christopher Alexander describes this relationship between humans and our environments as a porous relation. We are not affected, says Alexander, merely by each other and the numerous activities surrounding us or in which we engage each day. As embodied creatures we exist within a complex web of relations and events, both human and nonhuman, which affects the character of a place and, accordingly, the character of its inhabitants. We are the places where we are.

> The sunshine shining on the windowsill, the wind blowing in the grass are events too—they affect us just as much as social events. Any combination of events, which has a bearing on our lives—an actual physical effect on us—affects our lives.[50]

When that first glimmer of spring descends upon the faces of northern bodies bludgeoned by the cold of winter, a transformation occurs. A new disposition is acquired, perhaps resurrected. The snow begins to be perceived differently and the longer days stir up life in us all over again, and no matter how many times this cycle repeats itself it is ever new and always transformative. Ideas we often recognize as objectively occurring in our minds are actually contingent, richly attached to the world we inhabit, a world as simple and complex as the spaces and people in which and with whom *we live and move and have our being*. If we desire to understand the life that occurs in a building or town, says Alexander, "we must therefore try to understand the structure of the space itself."[51] We are affected and affecting, and recognizing our affective nature is the first step toward understanding how we come to perceive the world through prayer.

---

50. Christopher Alexander, *The Timeless Way of Building* (Berkeley: Center for Environmental Structure, 1979), 64.
51. Ibid., 74.

CHAPTER 7

Habitats of Grace

I am the space where I am.

Noël Arnaud

Our surroundings affect our disposition, even our aptitude. Architect Jan Gehl has observed that people walk more quickly in front of buildings with blank façades, as if trying to escape their blandness.[52] Psychologists James Danckert and Colleen Merrifield have found in their work on cognitive neuroscience that people who visually take in a "boring" environment, for instance the plain frontage of a Walmart store or the shadowy glass exterior of a Whole Foods, develop increased levels of cortisol, the stress hormone related to heart disease and diabetes.[53] These stark storefronts make us anxious. Not only this, but Canadian psychologist Donald Hebb has discovered that rats living in enriched environments are markedly more intelligent than those living in more spartan environs, which we find in the human sphere, too.[54]

---

52. Ellard, *Places of the Heart*, 109.
53. Ibid., 110.
54. Ibid., 114-115.

Just as Sam and Ellie Cluett take on the decorum of their 1885 home, we similarly grow with and relate to others relative to the spaces we regularly inhabit. This obviously extends well beyond church buildings; however, for our purposes, it is important to note that our spaces of prayer affect us. They register emotionally on our lives. They touch our relationships with others, how we relate to God, even how we relate to creation. And while we would not want to make a direct causal link between a particular house of prayer and what we individually believe about God, liturgical spaces are inseparable from how we come to perceive God and others.

Believing in God is intimately bound up in what the sociologist Marcel Mauss refers to as our *habitus*.[55] A *habitus* is a kind of subconscious bodily comportment that gives rise to a particular way of perceiving the world—a way of making meaning in and of the world. *Habitus* names a whole host of embodied movements in relation to people, places, and things, and the effects our movements have on how we relate to our environments, as well as how our environments affect how we move.

Space matters. My sense of self and others is always relative to the places where I live and move. Beautiful environs do actually increase intelligence, because they stimulate our imaginations. In a world of architectural efficiency, where aesthetics is often sacrificed for functionality, it should come as no surprise that perhaps the most common statement made about many of our older churches, those with real wood and much stained glass, is that "it's so peaceful." As a priest serving in a church built in 1866, where dark wood dominates the atmosphere and rich, stained glass fills the room, there is a palpable sensation that touches the worshiper when she walks in the door. The exterior of the church "looks like a church," and upon walking inside there is a distinct sense of entering a timeless dimension—a new orientation to time. A quantum leap

---

55. Marcel Mauss, "Techniques of the Body," in *Techniques, Technology and Civilisation*, ed. Nathan Schlanger (New York: Durkheim Press, 2011), 77-95; see also Talal Asad, *Genealogies of Religion: Discipline and Reasons of Power in Christianity and Islam* (Baltimore: Johns Hopkins University Press, 1993), esp. 55-79; and Pierre Bourdieu, *The Logic of Practice,* trans. Richard Nice (Stanford: Stanford University Press, 1990), 52-65.

occurs when we enter spaces clearly designed to be houses of prayer. This isn't to suggest that differently stained wood and plain glass are not fit for spaces of prayer; rather, it is simply to note the reality that there is a relational dynamic between us and the spaces where we pray. These spaces do affect our prayers. Space affects how we grow to speak and listen to God. Churches affect how we relate to God and others.

People and buildings do not have separate lives. Whether we like it or not, we live lives relative to the places where our lives happen. As Alexander further notes, "There is no aspect of our lives which is not governed by these patterns of events . . . *And indeed, the world does have a structure, just because these patterns of events which repeat themselves are always anchored in the space.*"[56]

Consider prayer as the *dominant habitus* of the church. Prayer and the movements of a church's liturgy have given rise to certain ecclesial structures. These buildings over time give shape to our lives and condition our imaginations. The more we pray in these spaces the more they affect our perception of God and others. The space of prayer is an emotional space. It is not surprising, for instance, that a historic church tends to house a more "traditional" form of worship. Nor is it at all astonishing that a church that gathers in a warehouse has a praise band and utilizes a projector for song lyrics, Bible verses, or video clips during its service. Spaces are conducive to certain forms of behavior, certain forms of prayer. Without arguing the validity of one form over another it is important to note the contrast between these differing spaces.

In the warehouse building of the modern church, it is typical that everything is completely bare. There are no windows, whether stained or clear glass; there is often a stage at the center; and the seating is generally arranged as an auditorium, encircling the platform or amphitheater style. The purpose of the design is to relieve the worshiper from all distractions, directing their attention to what is happening on stage or at the center, be it a song of praise, a Bible verse projected on a screen, or the preacher delivering a sermon.

---

56. Alexander, *The Timeless Way of Building,* 69, italics original.

In a traditional space of worship (and by traditional I refer to a cross- or dome-shaped church), the room is filled with a variety of colors, smells, and textures. Rather than metal stacking or folding chairs there are hardwood pews, or perhaps no pews at all. Hardwood pews are not the most comfortable; however, they are aesthetically pleasing to the touch and to the eye, more so than metal or plastic chairs. From a design perspective, these pews are relatable—they are porous. However uncomfortable they may be, we feel connected to them. The center aisle of a cruciform church creates a direct path to the altar in the sanctuary at the head, focusing our attention not so much on what the preacher may say from the pulpit, which is off to the side, but on what God is doing at the center. The preacher is expected to have something to say worth hearing; however, what God is doing in worship is the focal point. As important as the homily may be, it pales in comparison to the gift of life we receive from Christ in the Eucharist.

Movement within this space, as opposed to the movement in a warehouse church, has a cyclical feel. We are caught up in the Spirit's procession and return from and to the Father and Son, and throughout the liturgy parishioners enter and return, with Christ, to and from the throne room of God—the sanctuary. In a warehouse church the direction is almost always from the center toward the people, frequently moving in a unilateral direction. There is a certain passivity and inaccessibility created by the architecture itself, reinforced by the drama unfolding center stage.

Now, my bias is obvious, but what I hope is clear is that the worship of a people is relative to their space of worship. Each space creates certain conditions of possibility, and at the end of the day space always wins. The warehouse space designed for temporary occupancy will naturally give rise to a sense of worship that is temporary. Prayer does not linger in the warehouse when the service ends. Prayer becomes limited to the particular time at which the service is actively occurring. Porous spaces filled with relatable textures, aromas, and organic materials, however, encourage worshipers to return even outside set times for prayer. Why? In these spaces prayer is inscribed in the walls. Prayer lingers in these porous spaces in such ways that we can actually feel their resonance. Such spaces elicit something from us. We experience a visceral connection between the movement of worship and the space itself, which beckons our continuous return.

In one space worship is static; in another it is dynamic. In a warehouse the worship has a clear beginning and end; in a historic church we feel part of a continuum. In a porous space, liturgical acts soak into the walls and pews and a coherence occurs between the space and the action. Prayer inhabits the space as the building itself is gathered into the eternal liturgy of God. Shaped by its *dominant habitus*—the cross— the space retains a residue of the Spirit's procession and return from and to the Father and Son, in which we too are gathered. This spiritual residue is the abiding presence of the Holy. It's not just the organic material; rather, organic material becomes intimately connected to the divine energy, mingled together with the grace of God.

This is something we often miss in a world of plastic and synthetic. Organic materials are relatable. For instance, design studies have shown that people who have offices filled with real wood furniture and leather chairs are more creative and more productive than their counterparts who sit on faux leather or plastic at metal desks. Those whose offices are filled with natural lighting, real wood, and leather chairs are also more apt to engage their colleagues. Architecture affects our ability to be open to "an outside." It affects our relationships. Some spaces incline us to relate to others in collegial or friendly ways while others move us to behave competitively. As we begin to think more deeply about prayer it is crucial to recognize and name how our environments call us to attention. We are compelled to speak and relate to God and others through the places where we dwell, especially the places we inhabit most.

It is important, therefore, to emphasize that what the worshiper or wanderer experiences upon entering a sacred space, steeped as it is in the procession and return of God, is a tangible and sensible structure that is more than just a relatable space. It is a space intended for God to linger. The sense of divinity we feel upon entering is not accidental. God is there, and God is there in a way different than God's presence on the golf course or at the grocery store or in a sterile environment. A distinct, incarnate action occurs in liturgical space that orients the building itself to God, in a way that no other structure is oriented. What we experience in these divinely oriented houses of prayer is a space that reorients us to the divine—to the presence of God in the world.

CHAPTER 8

The Lamp of the Body

Prayer is really our whole life toward God . . .

Evelyn Underhill

What we've been describing is the reality that we are embodied creatures. Memory is likewise embodied. For instance, my teenage daughter often runs outside when it rains; she simply loves to run around and dance in the rain. She doesn't have a disorder (that we know of); she remembers the many times she and I would go outside and play in the showers of water when she was a child. The rain falling upon her skin reattaches her to the joyful memory of playing outside with her brother and me as Amanda sat on the porch laughing and smiling at us. These memories are attached to the feeling we experience when the rain touches our skin, and are attached to the smiles and laughter we have experienced on numerous occasions. Now a teenager, Aydah's the one inviting me to go outside to walk in the rain.

The wetness of the rain, the tickling of grass, or the grit of sand between our toes reminds—brings to the surface of our consciousness—experiences we have had in relation to these tangible realities. Our *haptic* nature, as the Finnish architect Juhani Pallasmaa describes our nature as embodied creatures, is charged by any number of experiences that bring to life in us prior experiences. "All the senses, including vision,

are extensions of the tactile sense."[57] What we *know* is first apprehended through our *haptic* sense—through our bodies. Everything is in some way an extension of our sense of touch. In our technologically advanced age much attention has been given to the overwhelming influence various devices have on our imaginations and behavior. What is most often stressed, perhaps leading to renewed emphasis on mindfulness, is the matter of physical presence. Am I really present with others when I am not physically there? Am I truly present when I am in the same room but my head, hands, eyes, and ears are directed toward the tiny handheld screen of my cell phone?

We have a "cell phone station" in our home, where everyone's phones are docked, and during mealtimes they are set to "do not disturb" or turned off altogether. Why? Our devices make it difficult for

---

57. Juhani Pallasmaa, *The Eyes of the Skin: Architecture and the Senses* (Chichester: Wiley-Academy, 2005), 10.

us to be present with the people in the room. If I'm sitting at the dinner table with friends and family while everyone is on their phones, are we really together? Every time I am out with my daughter and we pass a couple sitting at a restaurant or café table and witness the all too common sight of people staring at their devices (or worse, when one person is on a device and the other waits to be noticed), I say to Aydah, "If you are ever on a date with a young man and he pulls out his cell phone, get up and leave. Call me and I'll come pick you up." I say this with a hint of sarcasm, but I do mean what I say. The last thing I want for my daughter is for her to be with someone who ignores her or who attends to whoever or whatever is not there. Cell phones are a problem; however, they are symptomatic of this world's *dominant habitus*. We all suffer from attention deficit, to one degree or another, and while there are those who have real chemical deficiencies, the rest of us simply lack the discipline to attend to one thing at a time. This takes practice. A distracted mind reveals a distracted body.

In the Gospels of Matthew and Luke, Jesus reminds us that "the eye is the lamp of the body."[58] It is important to note that this understanding of "lamp" or vision is entirely different from how we understand the operation of the eye in modern society. We tend to limit the scope of vision to consumption. That is, the eye takes in a person's surroundings or the images we see. This understanding of vision comes to us from René Descartes, who, in the seventeenth century, scraped off the eye of a bull to look through it, discovering the mystery of human sight. Descartes's investigation showed that if you look through the back of an eye the world is inverted, which the mind, says Descartes, mysteriously turns right side up, so that we don't think we're walking on air. What is important to note is that after Descartes and the Scientific Revolution, the eye begins to move in a single direction. However, when Jesus is walking about the earth, and in the centuries that precede and follow him in human history, the eyes do more than take in their surroundings. The eye, as Christ says in the gospels, emits light. As with headlights on a

---

58. Matt. 6:22-23; Luke 11:34-36.

car, the eye shines light on what lies before, and the "brightness" of our light determines how much we actually see.[59]

This also sheds new light on Jesus's claim that it is not what goes into a person that defiles, but what comes out that defiles.[60] We are constantly taking things in. We cannot help but absorb the world around us. Nevertheless, without some form of *askesis*[61] we will only emit what we absorb. What is cast from our eyes, in other words, will merely be what we have taken in from our surroundings. All the judgments, anxiety, hate, suffering, gain at the expense of another, and every other vice to which we are exposed on any given day are constantly at work on our sensibilities. Even if we are not actively engaged in any of these vices that lead us away from Christ, they nonetheless affect who we are and how we perceive people, places, and things. Without habits that continually turn our attention to Christ, the light by which we see the world will not be the brightness of Christ. Instead, we will cast a dim shadow on the world. In the process, we will scarcely see Christ. When this happens, our neighbors appear before us as enemies. When this happens, the hungry seem to us as people "milking the system." When this happens, the homeless appear to be a burden, rather than God's gift entrusted to our care. Moving through life without the light of Christ beaming forth from our bodies, we will find ourselves stumbling, bumping into everyone and everything everywhere we go, on guard with our neighbors, avoiding the stranger, and continually finding ways to keep "outsiders" from access to resources we deceive ourselves to be scarce, or worse, ours alone.

The Prayer for Guidance in the BCP is a marvelous prayer that urges us to see all things with the light of Christ.

O God, by whom the meek are guided in judgment, and light riseth up in darkness for the godly: Grant us, in all our doubts and uncertainties, the grace to ask what thou wouldst have us to do, that the

---

59. For an interesting exploration of vision throughout history, see Authur Zajonc, *Catching the Light: The Entwined History of Light and Mind* (New York: Bantam Books, 1993).
60. Matt. 15:11.
61. *Askesis* (ἀσκήσεως), from which we get "ascetic," calls attention to the life of self-discipline—discipleship as an embodied orientation to our true love, God.

Spirit of wisdom may save us from all false choices, and that in thy light we may see light, and in thy straight path may not stumble; through Jesus Christ our Lord. Amen.[62]

This prayer tells us something about the character of those who see with the light of Christ. Such persons are meek. They don't have all the answers. They even have doubts. Yes, Christians are uncertain—especially about themselves. Yet in the midst of uncertainty and doubt followers of Christ rely on grace. Christians do not limit themselves to what they see by their own light, or what is immediately at hand. Seeking the spirit of wisdom they patiently wait for the light of Christ to shine upon the path of God, so that they remain on the path and do not stumble.

The image we have is twofold. The light of Christ gives light to our eyes, so that what enters our field of vision is visible with the brightness of Christ—the vision of humility and forgiveness. At the same time, Christ is also the light that shines over all things, illumining everything like the sun on a clear summer day. Here the light of Christ that is outside meets the light of Christ within as we are enjoined to the vision of God by this coalescing—this comingling—of lights, which is in fact the one light of God. We are active bearers of a light that is not our own.[63]

This vision is akin to what happens when we see rainbows. A rainbow is a natural wonder that occurs when the light of the sun is refracted by tiny droplets of water in the sky. Rain, or water off a lake or ocean, functions like a prism, dispersing the rays of sunlight and revealing the beautiful colors of nature. Without water we do not see the multiplicity of colors shining from the sun, yet water reveals that there is more to sunlight than what we are able to see on a clear day.

To see with the light of Christ is to become a prism of Christ. When we see with the light of Christ, drenched with the baptism of Christ, the overwhelming ray of God that gives light to the world is refracted in our bodies and we see a world of color, a world of harmonious difference. We do not see homogeneity or sameness; rather, we see Christ

---

62. BCP, 832.
63. See Rowan Williams, *The Edge of Words* (New York: Bloomsbury Publishing Plc., 2014), 111.

in the multiplicity. We see Christ in every person, place, or thing as they are alighted by Christ and not as they are judged according to my dim perception. At the same time, when the light of Christ coalesces in me I too become beautiful—beautifully colored—not because I am attractive or always say the right thing; rather, I emit the rainbow of God's promise, inclining others to see more than the singularities of age, race, gender, or any other worldly division we might conjure.

To recap: whatever my skin—my body—attends to is what governs my knowledge, awareness, even my memory. *Knowledge comes through contact.* What I *know* accords with how my body is conditioned to connect with (or disconnect from) people, places, and things.

How then do we condition our bodies in prayer? How do we discipline our bodies to be connected—yoked, to use biblical terminology—with Christ and detached from the chances and changes of this fleeting world? What are the movements by which we are to pattern our lives, so as to inhabit prayer—to inhabit our bodies—more deeply and become a prism of Christ?

CHAPTER 9

Apprehending God in My Body

God utters me like a word containing a partial thought of himself.

Thomas Merton

Think about the many ways we worship. My own devotion is more Anglo-Catholic in form. Having lived as a seminarian at Nashotah House Theological Seminary, the Anglo-Catholic wing of the Episcopal Church, I learned a distinct pattern of prayer and devotion. It is customary at Nashotah to observe certain gestures during the numerous services of prayer occurring each day at the House. When the name of Jesus is spoken, faculty and seminarians alike make a simple bow of the head in reverence. In certain passages of scripture, where Jesus's name is invoked several times, it can be a comical sight as heads bob up and down all across the chapel. In the midst of this hilarity there is an awareness that Jesus's name is not simply thrown about willy-nilly. It commands attention; it elicits a distinct posture from its hearers; and somewhere in the midst of this divine comedy the prayerful align their bodies to the language of revelation.

Walking before the altars that line the Chapel of St. Mary the Virgin, professors and seminarians make a reverent bow from the waist, to acknowledge that the tables they pass are not just any tables. They are places where God has made and continues to make incarnation available to our bodies. Places where God wills "to bring about the mystery of his embodiment."[64] Before the Corpus Christi altar in the chapel, where the body of Christ lies in a monstrance, the faithful genuflect, kneeling before Christ who is present through the host. No one is prostrating themselves before mere manna.[65] The gesture is a total recognition that this is food that sustains to immortality. Sacramental belief is bound up together with the gestures of belief, and in the process of reverencing the name of Christ, the altar of Christ, the body of Christ, we become Christ as our bodies are reconditioned to perceive Christ in all things and all people.

Imagine a life so disciplined by prayer and prayerful gestures that we begin bowing to the Christ in each other. St. Ignatius, the great bishop of Antioch, reminds us that we are to reverence a bishop as if reverencing Christ. This is not about submission to a human authority; rather, it is about honoring Christ in each person, honoring Christ in the bishop who serves the church *as* Christ. When we revere our bishops we remind them and ourselves that they and we are participants in a body that transcends our mortal bodies. Together we are the body of Christ. In a world patterned by individualism it is difficult to see such reverent acts as more than subservient postures. While there has been much evidence of clergy abusing their power in the history of the church, we Christians are nonetheless called to take on postures of devotion that manifest our hidden nature as portions of God—the *imago Dei*. It is easy for clergy and laity alike to forget that we are this image when we fail to pattern our bodies accordingly. We fail to apprehend God in the world, in ourselves, and in each other when we fail to acknowledge the sensibility of God through postures of humility.

---

64. Maximus Confessor, "Ambiguum 7," in *On Difficulties in the Church Fathers: The Ambigua*, trans. Nicholas Constas, vol. I (Cambridge: Harvard University Press, 2014), 1084D.
65. John 6.

The Prayer of Humble Access is perhaps the best prayer we pray that connects us to this reality.

> We do not presume to come to this thy Table, O merciful Lord, trusting in our own righteousness, but in thy manifold and great mercies. We are not worthy so much as to gather up the crumbs under thy Table. But thou art the same Lord whose property is always to have mercy. Grant us therefore, gracious Lord, so to eat the flesh of thy dear Son Jesus Christ, and to drink his blood, that we may evermore dwell in him, and he in us. Amen.[66]

Think about these words: *we do not presume* and *we are not worthy.* The prayer is a total acknowledgment that the immortal food we eat, the life we live, and the grace we receive are all gifts from God. We haven't earned it; we don't deserve it; yet God, *whose property is always to have mercy*, graces us with God's own life-giving presence. How these words register on us, however, depends on our physical posture. With exceptions for the aged, infirm, or differently abled, if we are simply sitting or standing when we pray this prayer our bodies contradict the words we pray. If I do not take on a posture of humility, my body makes presumptions for me; my body bears witness to a worth I cannot claim. Apart from a posture of humility this prayer becomes abstracted words on a page, as I deceive myself into believing I, apart from mercy and grace, am worthy of God's attention.

There are, however, times when we are called to take on a posture of worthiness, especially during Eastertide. The fifty days of Easter is a time to stand in the grace of God as we learn to inhabit the generosity of salvation. Eucharistic Prayer B is especially fitting for Eastertide for this reason.

> . . . For in these last days you sent him to be incarnate from the Virgin Mary, to be the Savior and Redeemer of the world. In him, you have delivered us from evil, and *made us worthy to stand before you.*[67]

---

66. BCP, 337.
67. BCP, 368, italics mine.

We give thanks to the Creator of the universe who in Christ has made us worthy to stand. Traditionally, during the fifty days of Easter there is no confession of sin on Sundays, and the expectation is that everyone would stand throughout the whole of the Eucharistic Prayer. This is to align our bodies with the fullness of Christ's redeeming work, bringing us out of error into truth. For those whose pious devotion compels them to kneel throughout the Eucharistic canon, their posture of humility, while noble, betrays in this instance the work of God in Christ. When Christ calls us to stand we should stand. When we are acknowledging our dependence and utter contingency upon grace and mercy it is fitting to kneel, as in the season of Lent. Our posture needs to match the language of our prayers. The language of humility with a posture of worthiness relieves humble words of their meaning. The language of worthiness met with a posture of humility stifles our relationship with God through a kind of psychological distancing.[68]

Perception follows posture. How our bodies move conditions how we grow to understand the meanings of words. Language is bound together with bodily movement, which long predates speech. As humans we gesture before we speak; we touch before we talk. All is language, but language is first and foremost nonverbal. Owning this reality about human nature is a crucial first step toward inhabiting and being inhabited by conversation with God—that is, prayer. As Christians we worship the God whose movement is none other than the Word of God at work in us. And unlike our own speech, where words are separable from deeds, God's Word is always incarnate. Word and deed in God are inseparable. Image and likeness are one in Christ. Our task is to become in likeness what we are in image,[69] learning to move as Christ so that our speech conforms to the movement of grace in the world.

---

68. See Lisa Feldman Barrett, *How Emotions Are Made: The Secret Life of the Brain*, (New York: Houghton Mifflin Harcourt, 2017), esp. 175-198.
69. See chapter 1.

CHAPTER 10

Grammar that Glorifies

The forms and materials which the poet uses, his images and the meanings he would give to those images, his perceptions, what is evoked, invoked or incanted, is in some way or other, to some degree or other, essentially bound up with the particular historic complex to which he, together with each other member of that complex, belongs.

David Jones

Recognizing that the language of prayer is first a posture and second a word allows us to rethink what language is altogether. Language apps on our phones have been quite helpful in this regard. Learning a secondary language has been difficult in modern society. It has been difficult because we are often taught grammatical rules before we learn how to speak the language. However, our primary language is something we acquire through exposure and repetition. Language apps do not teach us the rules of grammar; they expose us to word associations with images on the screen, just as we learned our primary language growing up. Our parents never sat down with a dictionary or the *Chicago Manual of Style* to teach us to talk; they pointed at an apple and said "apple." We learned how to speak by association. Before anyone ever spoke to us they first held us, fed us, smiled at us, laughed with us, and tossed us in the air, and through it all we learned powerful associations about what a parent is, what it means to be their child, what it means to be alive. We learned tones of speech before we learned which words are to be spoken. We learned words by hearing them over and over again and saying them terribly wrong until our patterns of speech matched what we heard spoken.

A subtle shift occurs, however, as we are being taught to read. Billy Collins notes in his poem "First Reader" that our parents and teachers redirect our attention from the pictures that showed the story to the words lined across the page. "They wanted us to look but we had looked already / and seen the shaded lawn, the wagon, the postman . . . / we were forgetting how to look, learning how to read."[70]

When the printed word becomes our focus we begin, even accidentally, to separate words from actions. We learn objectivity. As science infiltrates our imaginations through the printed word we disassociate word from deed. We begin to forget that language, like baseball, is caught before it is taught. In the same manner, we learned to pray not by someone instructing us on what words to use or how to use them. We knelt in the pew or at the altar rail. We held hands at the dinner table. We closed our eyes, because we know that God doesn't hear us unless our eyes are closed.

When the disciples said to Jesus, "Teach us to pray," Jesus did not say, "Here's a manual on prayer," or "Take this Book of Common Prayer and study it." Jesus said, "Pray in this way: 'Our Father. . . .' " Yet before Jesus says any of this, Jesus first goes off alone to pray. Jesus first reveals the need to frequent the Temple and synagogue to be present with God. It is only after acquiring the habit of being present before the Father that we can know what it means to say, "Our Father." It is only after walking around with Jesus feeding the hungry, healing the sick, comforting and caring for those left for dead on the side of the road that we can begin to say, "Our Father." The language of prayer is a movement before it is a word.

In other words, prayer is a movement—prayer moves us. I witnessed this movement firsthand when I was a child growing up in the church.

---

70. Billy Collins, "First Reader," in *Sailing Alone Around the Room: New and Selected Poems* (New York: Random House Inc., 2001), 39.

Brother Baker, as I was taught to call him, would always wander around the church waving a white hanky, shaking everyone's hands. As a child, I found this terribly amusing. As a teenager, it only got funnier. My friends and I used to bet Summit Bars on how long it would take Brother Baker to get up and start his procession around the church. I almost always won. The liturgical tradition of my childhood, which was the Church of the Nazarene, always began with a hymn, a prayer, another hymn, a special song, an altar call, the offertory, the sermon, maybe another altar call, a repeatable hymn, and some form of passing the Peace mixed in between. Brother Baker always stood up somewhere in the middle of the special hymn, and almost always during the final altar call. Like taking candy from a baby.

I remember none of the sermons I heard growing up, which, as a preacher, I find entirely disconcerting. But I will never forget Brother Baker. As an adult, I miss having someone wandering around the church telling people how much God loves them. I miss seeing prayer physically move someone out of their pew to speak a word of truth. With no Brother Bakers wandering around in our churches—people captivated by prayer who are crazy enough to tell everyone that Jesus loves them— we are liable to forget that prayer is a movement. This is by no means to suggest that the little old lady sitting in the pew thumbing her rosary has no idea what prayer is. Brother Bakers of the world will always be the exception. However, these persons remind us that prayer inhabits us; prayer bubbles up within and calls us to attention—to action. Prayer is a form, a habit, before it is an utterance.

I am now an Episcopalian. There is little risk of Episcopalians standing up in the middle of the service to wander around with hankie in hand. We have the occasional child roaming the aisle, which is altogether wonderful, yet there is a movement of prayer that is distinctly Anglican— distinctly Episcopalian. It is often referred to as Episcopal calisthenics. There is a procession and return that patterns the movement of prayer among the faithful in Catholic expressions of liturgy. The procession of the cross guides us into prayer, and at the end of the liturgy it ushers us out into the world. We follow the cross to Christ at the opening procession; we follow the cross to the gospel as the Word of God enters the nave, into the belly of the church; we follow the cross to the homily; at the offertory we follow Christ to the cross as we lay ourselves, with our wealth and talents and with Christ, on the table for consecration; our crucified and resurrected selves return to us with Christ in the Eucharist; and the cross of resurrection leads us out into the world at the recession as we are sent, following the cross, into the world to proclaim the good news of God in Christ.

Congregants may not get out of their pews to wander around the church but we do bow before the cross as it passes before us, acknowledging our participation in its procession. As a mark of our humility, we reverence the cross as if reverencing Christ, which gives meaning to our words when we say, "Glory to you, Lord Christ." Bowing before the cross is not accidental; it is the pattern of glorifying God in our bodies.

When we fast we acknowledge that our hunger for Christ is our true craving. These bodily disciplines are movements that make our words sensible. Living without chocolate during Lent is *not* fasting. Abstaining from a meal, calculating the cost of the meal we would have eaten, and then giving this food or money to someone who is hungry—someone for whom missing a meal is not an option—is prayer-formed fasting. Disconnecting from this divine form of generosity disconnects our words from the thoughts and deeds of Christ—disconnects us from the action of Christ. Fasting is one of the many ways we are to follow the cross in procession before the world. This is what speaking the language of Christ looks like. This is what our scripted prayers call us to. They are not there to stymie faith. The words on the page are not there to stifle creativity. Rather, they open us to the creative action of God in Christ, so that our bodies come mutually to inhabit and be inhabited by their procession and return in us with the heavenly host.

Our prayers will not be "felt," however, if we do not move with them—if we do not let them stir us to make peace with our neighbor. If we do not forgive those who sin against us, praying to God, "forgive us our sins as we forgive those who sin against us" bears no weight. We disconnect ourselves from the forgiveness of Christ when we are not "in love and charity with our neighbors," or do not "intend to lead a new life following the commandments of God."[71] It's easy to lose sight of grace and forgiveness when we read them as scripts on the page, rather than as the pattern of Christian living. We must begin to recognize that we do not so much pray these prayers as they pray us—*they pray us into being.*

---

71. BCP, 330.

CHAPTER 11

The Timeless
Way of Being

If a man wants God to hear his prayer quickly, then before he prays for anything else, even for his own soul, when he stands and stretches out his hands towards God, he must pray with all his heart for his enemies. Through this action God will hear everything that he asks.

Sayings of the Desert Fathers

I had been serving as the director of spiritual formation, responsible for the formation of both adults and children. The adults were easier to manage, but the children were by far the more interesting. During my six-year tenure, I worked with parishioners to build a program that was strong and engaging. It got off to a slow start, as it took me a while to adjust to some deep-rooted personalities in the church; however, we turned a corner somewhere along the way and things came alive. The church was increasing in families, baptisms, income, and outreach. Things were going well.

As I began my fifth year of ministry, the rector and I met to review how things were going, and he informed me that I needed to make a transition. I was caught off guard. He was kind about it, giving me plenty of time to find a new position.

I was able to secure a position as a hospice chaplain, which would prove tremendously beneficial in my own journey and spiritual growth, all the while completing a necessary aspect of my candidacy with the diocese. I needed hospice and, it turns out, they needed me. After some time away we returned to the church as parishioners, so that our son could continue singing in the boys' choir. We sat in the pew and worshiped, for the first time in a long time, as a family. At first it was awkward, but this faded swiftly and the parishioners were quite gracious.

One Sunday, following a swift departure of the new assistant who had taken over the position, the rector addressed the congregation, saying, "She's done a great job, coming into a very difficult situation when things had really fallen apart." I was livid and Amanda, my wife, was in tears. Being a childhood educator, Amanda had been integral in helping me build the children's ministry program, which had been thriving—nowhere close to falling apart. If our son had not been sitting in the choir we may have walked out of church, even though I hate when people do this.

When we got home from church that day, I expressed my frustration to Amanda and she her sadness to me. But then Amanda said something I didn't anticipate: "You need to meet with him and make things right." She was right. To this day I don't know what I did to make him feel the need to replace me in the position, and I'm not sure why he characterized my work the way he did. I invited him to meet with me, which we did that week. We met for lunch and I said to him quite plainly, "I don't know what I've done to hurt you, but whatever it is, I'm sorry. I don't understand what I may have done, and I don't understand why you said what you did, but whatever I've done, I'm sorry." "I see how what I said on Sunday could be perceived as a commentary on what you did," he replied. "It was not intended that way."

The conversation did not go much further. I did not walk away with the feeling of having reconciled. However, from that point on there was a noticeable shift in our relationship. He became one of my biggest supporters. His demeanor toward me was as if we had just met. He was starting afresh, and I was grateful for this strange reconciliation.

How would things be today if Amanda had not compelled me to meet with him? Would he know that things were amiss between us? Would I still be upset? The transition was a difficult time for my family and me. Nevertheless, the restored friendship between us is real, and I see him only in the light of the strange and unlikely reconciliation Christ makes available. This is what grace looks like. This is what Beloved Community looks like. This is how relationships are changed. Having our minds renewed by offering ourselves as a living sacrifice, we come to inhabit and to be inhabited by the love of God in Christ in our bodies. Grace restores relationships, rejuvenates friendships, and transforms, as Martin Luther King Jr. writes regarding the creation of Beloved Community, "opposers into friends."[72]

Turning opposers into friends can sound like far-fetched idealism, yet transfiguring our relationships *with God's help* is the call of Christ. This can be a difficult task, especially if the circumstances are beyond our control, e.g., if it involves our skin color, place of origin, etc. There is a young girl in our diocese who experienced an inherited form of racism after moving to rural Southern Tier in western New York. Alfina and her family moved to western New York from India; when she saw snow for the first time, she said it felt like being "a fairy in fairyland." Alfina's father is an Anglican priest. She and her family moved to America so that Abi, her father, could study theology and serve in an Episcopal church. Coming from India, which is a country flooded with cultural and religious diversity, to rural western New York was a culture shock to say the least. Alfina and her brother entered the local school system in an area predominantly occupied by rural, white Americans. Alfina's family *is* the racial diversity in their village.

---

72. Martin Luther King Jr., "The Role of the Church in Facing the Nation's Chief Moral Dilemma," 1957, Stanford University, accessed November 7, 2018, http://okra.stanford .edu/transcription/document_images/Vol04Scans/184_1957_The%20Role%20of%20 the%20Church.pdf.

Alfina stood out, not only because of the color of her skin, but also because of her clothes. Coming from India, where attire is much more colorful and traditional than the typical child wandering about American schools, it was hard not to spot Alfina in a crowd. Children are largely accepting of their peers, but children also carry with them the background and biases of their families and environments.

Before going to her new school, Alfina described her experience in America, "in this land of immigrants," as being "good and happy." This sentiment would soon change. Not long after her family had settled into their new environs and Alfina had begun school, a young girl in her class said to Alfina, "You are a terrorist!" As Alfina recalled the situation, her classmate's face was "red with hate and anger." "I did not know what to do," recounted Alfina. "Tears filled my eyes and my heart pounded loud. What did I ever do to her, to call me like that? I just wanted to run away into the restroom and cry. I was so embarrassed."

Hate comes in all shapes and sizes, but it doesn't just come from nowhere. It comes from a habitat of hate. Children are naturally inclined to share what they have. They learn from adults to say, "Mine." They learn from grown-ups to be childish instead of being children. Hate is learned; love is natural.

It wasn't long before the teacher learned of Alfina's encounter with the young girl. The situation was swiftly directed to the principal, who immediately contacted Abi, who rushed to the school to embrace his daughter. "As I saw him coming closer towards me, I wanted to cry but I did not because I don't want to make him sad," Alfina said. "My dad's face was glowing with love and joy instead of anger, and he embraced me with his smile. I immediately understood that he had forgiven my classmate and he asked me to forgive her with love." *And a little child shall lead them.*[73]

I am a pretty mild-mannered person. I like to think that I carry the peace of Christ wherever I go. But if someone directed this sort of hate toward my own daughter, I'm not so sure my initial response would be

---

73. Isa. 11:6.

forgiveness. Yet Alfina and her family know that the only way to end the cycle of hate in this world is to extend love, especially to those who hate us. When Alfina returned to school the next day the young girl apologized. "I forgave her," remarked Alfina, "and eventually we became friends." As it turns out, the young girl had come home from school after Alfina's arrival and told her parents about a new family that had moved to town. She informed her parents that Alfina had dark skin and that she was from India. "They must be terrorists," her father said. Apples rarely fall far from the tree. Only by the grace of God does someone pick up the apple and take it to good soil, which is exactly what Alfina and her family did. "It's not your fault," Alfina told the girl. "You only heard it from your dad."

This is what it looks like to inhabit the language of Christ in our bodies, in our relationships, and in the many places where violence occurs. Forgive us *as* we forgive, Jesus reminds us in the Lord's Prayer. When we separate our forgiveness from the forgiveness we have received, we separate the words of our prayers from a life of prayer—the words of forgiveness from a life of forgiving and being forgiven. Alfina and her family know that we cannot experience the peace of Christ apart from a life patterned by prayer and forgiveness. We will not be inhabited by Christ if we do not inhabit the way of Christ's prayer to *Our* Father. But when we step out in faith, extend grace, repent *and* forgive, the timeless way of prayer throws us into being, raising us to newness of life, as opposition comes to an end and friendship in Christ flourishes.

Conclusion

Give what you ask, O God, and ask it of me.

St. Augustine

When we are baptized we are asked several questions about what we will do with our baptism.

Will you continue in the apostles' teaching and fellowship, in the breaking of the bread, and in the prayers? Will you persevere in resisting evil, and, whenever you fall into sin, repent and return to the Lord? Will you proclaim by word and example the Good News of God in Christ? Will you seek and serve Christ in all persons, loving your neighbor as yourself? Will you strive for justice and peace among all people, and respect the dignity of every human being?[74]

Sometimes I think we take these questions for granted and move through them too quickly in our liturgies. Not unlike the Ten Commandments, these questions direct our attention to a life that is all about loving God *and* our neighbor. They remind us that we Christians are called to a dangerous adventure that begins with holding our heads underwater, which is never comforting. We've glamorized baptism a bit too much by sprinkling water over our heads. The Spirit still moves, but do we know that we have died?

---

74. BCP, 304-305.

When we say that we will "strive for justice and peace among all people, and respect the dignity of every human being," do we realize that this means respecting the dignity of those who have lost all respect for themselves—those who spread hate? Do we realize that this means respecting the Christ in those who hate us, so that they learn to recognize in themselves more than their hate? Following Christ in the way of forgiveness, where we reach out to forgive others before they reach out to repent, requires a humility that is difficult to muster. This is why we respond, "I will, *with God's help*." When we reach out for Christ in our enemies it is not because we are so great and strong so to do; rather, it means that the peace and forgiveness at work in us through Christ is reaching out to the Christ in our neighbors, so that the way of incarnate love is made manifest in our midst and we are strengthened in our inner being with power through God's Spirit.[75] In so doing Christ comes to dwell in our hearts through faith, as we are rooted and grounded in love.[76] As Paul writes to the Ephesians, his prayer is that they "may have the power to comprehend, with all the saints," including saints such as Alfina, "what is the breadth and length and height and depth, and to know the love of Christ that surpasses knowledge, so that [they] may be filled with all the fullness of God."[77] Christ is the one who accomplishes God's love in us, a love that reaches beyond what we might imagine to be possible—even transforming "opposers into friends."[78]

No one said this life would be easy. If anyone told you this they were lying. What we do know is that the Christ who is in us is greater than any evil at work in the world.[79] And we will know Christ by our love for one another, for this is how God is made manifest in our bodies.[80] It does, however, require that we become like little children.[81] Alfina is ten, but the faith at work in her is eternal. Her witness to the forgiveness of Christ

---

75. Eph. 3:16.
76. Eph. 3:17.
77. Eph. 3:18-19.
78. See n. 72 on p. 65.
79. 1 John 4:4b.
80. 1 John 4.
81. Matt. 18:3.

is what it looks like to be inhabited by Christ. She is an exemplar in the way of incarnate love.

Discussion Questions

1. Have you ever considered how your environments are shaping how you perceive God and others? How might the environments of your home, office, or school impact your relationships with others?

2. We often think that our eyes are used solely to take in our surroundings. What do you think about the biblical imagery that our eyes actually cast light upon the world, by which we perceive people, places, and things?

3. How might this deeper understanding of vision, whereby we see based on our habit of life, change your perception of others? In other words, if you see a person as a threat to your wellbeing, what about your habit of life might be imposing this perception of fear?

PART III

The Peace of Christ

"And with Thy Spirit."

You have heard that it was said to those of ancient times, "You shall not murder"; and "whoever murders shall be liable to judgment." But I say to you that if you are angry with a brother or sister, you will be liable to judgment; and if you insult a brother or sister, you will be liable to the council; and if you say, "You fool," you will be liable to the hell of fire. So when you are offering your gift at the altar, if you remember that your brother or sister has something against you, leave your gift there before the altar and go; first be reconciled to your brother or sister, and then come and offer your gift.

Matthew 5:21-24

CHAPTER 12

The Gift of Suffering

The sign of Christ is legible only if we read his human love and self-gift unto death as the manifestation of absolution love.

Hans Urs von Balthasar

Her name was Minerva. She was a hospice patient entrusted to my care when I was a young sapling in ministry and had no idea what I was doing. Minerva taught me what everyone learns in the process of serving those most in need—more often than not, it is we the servants who find ourselves entrusted to the care of those we serve. They have so much more to offer us than we have to offer them. This was certainly the case between Minerva and me, and I will never forget her, not simply because of her quite memorable name but because of the richness of her faith.

I had been asked to visit Minerva because the hospice nurse on my team was having difficulty getting her to take pain medication. Minerva was suffering from a form of intestinal cancer that had spread throughout her abdomen. The pain had become unbearable, making Minerva's last days harsh and difficult. Throughout her decline, however, Minerva refused to take pain medication, which baffled the nurse. "Nobody refuses pain medicine at this stage," the nurse told me.

When I visited Minerva, I asked her all the questions you're supposed to ask: Are you concerned that you won't be able to think clearly? Are you anxious about becoming addicted to the medication? Are you worried about side effects?

I will never forget her response. This petite woman from Spain, whose family had moved to Cuba when she was a little girl and later immigrated to the United States when she was a teenager, looked lovingly into my eyes, as one might gaze upon a toddler who can't seem to get the large, square block into the small, round hole. In a matter-of-fact tone, Minerva said to me: "If I take the pills, I will not suffer. If I do not suffer, I will have nothing to offer to God."

I've held the hand of many a dying person. I've witnessed terror in the face of impending death, true angst. I've seen many a peaceful death—death in the confidence that all will be well. But I've never seen faith quite like Minerva's. There was no anxiety in Minerva. There was no longing for something more, and no great anticipation in her eyes, as we might think of saints longing for heaven. What I saw in Minerva could only be described as trust.

If I've learned anything in two decades of ministry it is that trust is hard to come by. The difficulty, however, is our grave misunderstanding about what trust is. We tend to think of trust as something earned. We say, "I earned her trust" or "He hasn't earned my trust yet." When we think of trust as something earned by being trustworthy, trust becomes contractual, more like a bank mortgage. I sign this piece of paper. I make this monthly payment, and the bank and I trust each other to hold up our respective ends of the bargain. However, if one of us fails to keep the terms of the agreement I sue the bank or the bank takes my home. Contractual trust is not really trust at all.

Any parent of a teenager knows that trust is anything but earned. We do not wait for our children to earn our trust. If we did, no teenager would ever drive a car or perhaps ever leave the house. Sure, we trust that our children will wake up too early or keep us up late at night. But again, this is not the trust of which we speak. This is merely part of their obligation to deprive parents of peace and sleep whilst we raise them to adulthood. But our children do not earn our trust, at least not initially; rather, we trust our children in order that they might become trustworthy. Trust is first and foremost a gift. I can only earn another's trust to the extent that I am trusted. To receive it well is to become worthy of it. In other words, I am made worthy of another's trust not because I do something trustworthy but because I am trusted into becoming worthy by another's trust.

The primary example we have of trust as a gift is Jesus Christ. The Incarnation is not a test of our humanity, nor is it an interruption in the ordinary life of God. The Incarnation fulfills the union of divine and human natures begun in creation, and in the process of bringing creation to its natural end, God entrusts divinity to us. God in Christ *trusts us into trusting*. Without entrusting God's life to us we would be unable to trust God. It is in this sense that God does not love and redeem humanity despite our sinfulness or untrustworthiness; rather, God loves and redeems us because without the sustaining gift of love and redemption—without trusting us with God's own life—we would only be sinful and untrustworthy. We would be incapable of love, incapable of redemption, unable to entrust ourselves to the love and redemption of God in Christ.

This way of trust is the way of vulnerability. I make myself vulnerable when I share my life with another person. I tell them the good, the bad, and the ugly and trust that they will not use it against me.[82] In love, I give another person my life and remain confident in the act of self-offering that they will receive my trust as a gift, rather than deny my gift and thereby refuse friendship with me in love.

This is the way of the suffering servant, the way of the cross—the way of Christ. Yet we know that this form of trust, this way of vulnerability, ends with Jesus nailed to the cross. And whether or not it is the paradigm for fellowship in Christ, who wants that? We've all been betrayed. And the last thing we want to do with someone who has betrayed our trust is trust them—to entrust anything more to them. When Jesus prays in the Garden of Gethsemane, saying, "Father, if it is possible, let this

---

82. Simon Sinek, *Leaders Eat Last* (New York: Penguin Random House LLC, 2017), 61.

cup pass from me,"[83] he is praying to *Our* Father, "You know they can't be trusted." "Nevertheless," says Jesus, "even if you entrust me to them, I trust you."

The faith of Christ is the way of trustful obedience. It is crying out to God with open ears. Faith is inseparable from the form of listening that we saw earlier in *The Rule of Saint Benedict*. As listening bears an intent to act, faith bears the mark of Christ's obedience to the will of the Father. Faith is a matter of trusting the silence and self-offering of Christ enough to set aside what I want and to inhabit the way of vulnerability, even if I am likely to be betrayed. Why? For starters, what *I* know is not absolute. My reasoning and understanding, however thoughtful, patient, or grounded, is always limited; it is always contingent upon factors for which I can never fully account. Second, my knowledge is never determinative. What I know about a person in one instance does not determine how he or she will act in another. And I should never become a prophet for evil, not unlike the self-fulfilling prophecies of parents and teachers who refer to their child and student as a "bad child." Faith means trusting the vulnerability and self-offering of Christ to do its work in the other person, to do its work in me, and in the process to entrust the outcome to God, especially when the end result may be betrayal. Jesus did not stop trusting when the soldiers taunted him, spat on him, stripped him naked, and thrust nails into his hands and feet. Instead, Jesus continued in the way of forgiveness.

We don't know if any of the soldiers became converts that day. At least one seems to have changed his mind about Jesus's divinity, declaring, "Truly this man was God's Son,"[84] but at the end of the day we don't know if it "paid off." Did Pilate ever convert because of the forgiveness shown to him? How about Malchus, the temple guard whose ear Peter sliced off and Jesus healed? Or maybe the payoff is not the end result. Perhaps we never get to know if trusting the will of God is going to bring about the end we needed yet could not see, barring resurrection of course. This, it seems, is our dilemma. We trust, so long as the end

83. Matt. 26:39.
84. Matt. 27:54b.

result is better than we could have imagined. We trust, so long as we get what we wanted in the first place. We do not trust in order to become trusting—in order to become perfect in our self-offering, as Christ in his self-offering is perfect. We trust to the degree that we can anticipate something beneficial for ourselves. We separate sacrifice from trust, and in the process separate ourselves from Christ.

"People who know nothing of God and whose lives are centered on themselves," says Thomas Merton, "imagine that they can only find themselves by asserting their own desires and ambitions and appetites in a struggle with the rest of the world."[85] A life centered on ourselves is an atheistic life. Selfishness and atheism go hand in hand, and while not all who claim to be atheist are selfish, neither do all who claim to be Christian really believe in God. Just as there is no room for hate in the heart of Christ, neither is there any room for selfishness in God.

It is for this reason that suffering is a wise teacher. "Bodily weakness," writes Maximus Confessor, "is an education concerning our true dignity as a portion of God."[86] Contrary to modern inclinations toward the prosperity gospel, early Christians recognized that it was not health and wealth that revealed God's blessings; rather, it was weakness, poverty, and suffering that showed the way—the stuff of sermons on mountains. "Blessed be the poor in spirit . . . Blessed are those who mourn . . . Blessed are the pure in heart . . . Blessed are the peacemakers . . . Blessed are those who suffer for righteousness' sake. . . ."[87] When early Christians recounted the Sermon on the Mount they trusted what Jesus actually said, not a cozier, more guarded version of it. They believed these words to be true and began to see not how exciting it is to suffer, but that suffering is a faithful educator in the life beyond what we can experience in our mortal bodies. There is, rather, a new flesh, a new body for which our bodies groan. Suffering reminds us that this too shall pass away. Suffering and death are no longer a mark of our finitude but direct our attention to the infinite.

---

85. Merton, *New Seeds of Contemplation*, 47.
86. Maximus, "Ambiguum 7," 75.
87. Matt. 5.

Living in our midst are people who have become pupils of suffering, those who have learned to listen with their bodies, own their limitations, avoid the temptation to flee and, rather, settle in, inhabit mortality more deeply, and assimilate themselves, body and soul, to the self-offering of Christ. This is what I learned from Minerva, and from so many others in my life who have inhabited suffering with grace. Entrusting herself to God, Minerva was able to receive and offer her cancer-filled body with Christ in his suffering. By inhabiting her suffering body more deeply, Minerva was able to recognize the truth of her nature hidden in Christ. Because she did not flee from her suffering, she was able to see beyond it, transcending the weakness of her body through the body. Her life was an offering because she was attentive to suffering as an opportunity to become one with Christ. God did not give Minerva cancer, even if cancer became an occasion for her to inhabit the way of Christ. This is the nuance saintly people reveal to us. Even though sin and evil are absent of life, the patient way of suffering will transform sin and evil, *with God's help*—grace—into manifestations of the Holy, whereby we are enabled to know Christ more clearly, love Christ more dearly, and follow Christ more nearly.

CHAPTER 13

Suffering and Forgiveness

Very often we see what we expect to see and reject what does not fall within the parameters of our expectations or what we think is important.

Phoebe Caldwell

This way of suffering we've been describing is what Maximus Confessor refers to as "crucifying the world in our bodies." We are, says Maximus, proportionately more capable of knowing Christ in others and in ourselves to the degree that we live sacrificial lives. So what does this mean?

I served for three years as the chaplain of Saint James School, a co-ed, Episcopal boarding school in Hagerstown, Maryland. Like most boarding schools, students and faculty live a common life together. They eat together, learn together, and often pray together. Prayer and worship are at the heart of Saint James School, which in my mind sets it apart from secular boarding schools. There are no fewer than eleven opportunities each week for students and faculty to gather together for organized prayer at Saint James. (It's a bit like seminary with teenagers, only less mischief.) Five are compulsory, and the other six are optional. The chapel is physically and spiritually at the heart of Saint James School. To attend Saint James is to learn how to pray, all the while receiving a fine education.

This also means that Saint James is a bit unusual, especially with a priest as the headmaster and another priest as its chaplain, which means that there are always two people walking around campus in clericals. When visitors or newcomers come to campus this is often surprising, especially when the priest is teaching history, coaching, or announcing the basketball games—all in a collar, and sometimes cassock. On one occasion, the new head football coach's family had come to watch the season opener. There was nothing unusual about the game, except that at the end of the game Father Dunnan, the headmaster, walked onto the field and gathered the team at the center for prayer. This was customary at Saint James, but unusual for outsiders. When the new coach asked his daughter how she enjoyed the game and what she thought about the campus, she responded by saying how much she enjoyed the campus and that the game was fun. "They do have a strange mascot, though," she said. Her father, being the new coach, didn't realize Saint James had a mascot. "Where did you see a mascot?" he asked. "That guy that came down on the field at the end of the game dressed in black," she said. "That's a strange costume."

The young girl had never seen a priest before, but given that her dad was a football coach she had witnessed a mascot coming onto the field at the end of numerous games. In her mind, the priest was the mascot, which may not be so far from the truth.

This is what Maximus is saying when he tells us that we know Christ in proportion to bodily knowledge in the way of sacrificial love. What I habitually experience in my body is what conditions how I see, think, and believe. If worldly pleasures surround and fill my body, can I know the Christ whom the world hung on a cross, the Christ who has food to eat we know not of? It's a difficult question to wrestle with, largely because most people reading this book, including the one writing it, will not miss a meal today. Or, if we do, it is likely to be because we forgot to eat or because we chose to abstain.

Knowing Christ is akin to childbirth for those who do not bear children. At no point in my entire life will I accumulate enough knowledge to understand what Amanda went through when she gave birth to our children. I know my children. I love my children. While I would do any-thing for them I will never *understand* childbirth, even though I was in the birthing room. I am biologically incapable of such comprehension. I can appreciate the pain and joy involved; I can sympathize and hold the hand of my wife as she squeezes our children from her womb, rejoicing in new life, as I did with both of our children. Nevertheless, my knowledge of childbirth is limited to my own bodily experience of witnessing childbirth.

This is analogous to knowing Christ. My knowledge of Christ is proportionate to my active and bodily participation in the way of self-offering, humility, and love. It is proportionate to my embodied proximity to Christ. In this sense the saints are those who give birth to Christ in their bodies. I can study them, learn from them, watch them, but until I take up my own cross and inhabit daily the way of love I will only know Christ as a great teacher; I will not know Christ with the saints as friend and savior.

It is for this reason that those who have experienced real pain and suffering often have a greater aptitude for forgiveness. Suffering offers perspective. After my wife's heart surgery when she was only twenty-five, faced with real uncertainty and coming through on the other side with rejoicing, I began to experience the petty concerns of life as comical, however frustrating they may be. I did not find myself angry with the person who rear-ended me at an intersection in Ames, Iowa, because it was an accident and accidents happen; it pales in comparison to possibly losing my wife and becoming a single parent. One week after having our car repaired, Amanda "decided" to back into the neighbor's metal mailbox and the mailbox won. When she called to tell me what had hap-pened the first thing out of my mouth was, "You know that's a federal offense, right?" A damaged car no longer rises to the level of pain and suffering, and I wasn't about to become angry. It was too comical to cause anger. Nor was I going to pay to have the scratch fixed. It now serves as a continual reminder that stuff doesn't matter. I know what loss looks like; I have experienced real anxiety. And while I do *not* believe that one *must* suffer in order to be forgiving, it sure helps. We gain per-spective when we suffer in faith, not because the bar of human behavior is lowered, but because our empathy for others increases.

Pain and suffering invite us to become vulnerable. When we assume a posture of vulnerability, our suffering and pain bears us to the cross, as Christ is born in us, just as Minerva gave birth to Christ by the manner in which she received her cancer. It is here that we come to understand suffering less as an event that we passively undergo and more as a disposition of the soul. When I am vulnerable, the people around me, the land beneath my feet, and the circumstances that life throws my way all become gifts to be received, rather than threats to ward off. Through a posture of vulnerability I open my life, body and soul, as a dwelling place, a house of hospitality for friends, neighbors, even enemies. In my body I am opened to receive all things, even tragedy and illness, whether mine or another's, as gifts. I receive my enemy not as a foe, but as someone who is suffering. I open them to the transformation in which I am actively participating. Although suffering itself is not a gift, by grace and through a posture of vulnerability I can receive suffering and those who suffer. Instead of fighting a threat, I inhabit each with grace. Suffering and sufferer are transformed through my body as an incarnate act, proportionate to my inhabiting the way of the cross.

This is what it means to be open to suffering as an education of the soul. In his poem on sorrow, the poet Robert Browning Hamilton writes:

> I walked a mile with Pleasure; / She chattered all the way, / But left me none the wiser / For all she had to say. / I walked a mile with Sorrow / And ne'er a word she said; / But oh, the things I learned from her / When sorrow walked with me.[88]

Pleasure has a way of turning us in on ourselves. This is not to suggest that our lives should be empty of pleasure; however, it is not a faithful teacher. Nor is this to suggest that we should run after suffering. The saints have taught us well that those who seek to be martyrs more often than not deny the faith. Suffering cannot be treated as a goal or an end in itself; rather, it binds us together in the compassionate way of love, so long as we receive it with grace.

---

88. Robert Browning Hamilton, "Along the Road," in *First Loves*, ed. Carmela Ciuraru (New York: Scribner Poetry, 2000), 27.

CHAPTER 14

Before Offering Your Gift

When someone is trying to persuade me how deeply he has been wronged, there is always one vital thing left out: the other person.

Sebastian Moore

How we suffer and how we relate to those who have harmed us and those we have harmed are integral to the Christian life. There is a moment in our liturgy that keeps this reality present before us, week after week. It's the passing of the Peace. In many of our churches the Peace often looks more like glad-handing than it does a sharing of the Peace of Christ. In many churches the Peace seems to last forever, while in others we greet only those adjacent to us in our pews. It has become an "intermission" to the service, and instead of reconciling with those we have wronged or those who have wronged us, we say, "Good morning," or at best, "Peace," and we sit down. The formality of passing the Peace has a very specific purpose. We have gathered for liturgy; we have inwardly digested the word of God; we have participated in the priest's dialogue with scripture in the homily; we have confessed the faith, repented of our sins, and received absolution from God. The Peace now affords us, before we give our tithes and approach our Lord's table, the opportunity to be reconciled with our neighbor.

When I became a new rector, I was approached by a member of the congregation to mediate reconciliation between him and another parishioner; we'll call them Peter and Paul. I was humbled and immediately grateful for the opportunity. This is the stuff of priestly ministry, and here I was being actively approached to facilitate healing. Peter laid out his narrative, in which he expressed remorse for the friendship being severed, though he felt he had done what was right. He had acted justly, yet was aware that his actions bore consequences for the other parishioner's son. He was sorry and wanted to express his remorse and receive forgiveness from Paul.

I then visited with Paul and shared with him Peter's desire to be reconciled, expressing to him Peter's remorse and that he sought Paul's forgiveness. The matter was, in my mind, far from grave. Paul's son, John, was the coach of a local sports team. Peter did not feel as though John was treating the students very well, and that everyone was suffering in the process. Peter also had seniority at school to request that he become the head coach the following year. Peter did not go behind John's back, but went directly to John, expressed his concerns, and told John he was going to appeal to become the coach next year. As aforesaid this caused a rift between Peter and Paul. Many years had passed. It still weighed on Peter and he wanted to make things right and be reconciled.

In the process of inviting Paul to meet with Peter and work through the pain and be reconciled, Paul said quite plainly to me, "That's never going to happen. That's one I'll take to my grave."

When Jesus teaches his disciples how they are to seek reconciliation, *assuming* that his followers would from time to time be at odds with each other, he tells them to go straight to the source.

> If another member of the church sins against you, go and point out the fault when the two of you are alone. If the member listens to you, you have regained that one. But if you are not listened to, take one or two others along with you, so that every word may be confirmed by the evidence of two or three witnesses. If the member refuses to listen to them, tell it to the church; and if the offender refuses to listen even to the church, let such a one be to you as a Gentile and a tax collector. Truly I tell you, whatever you bind on

earth will be bound in heaven, and whatever you loose on earth will be loosed in heaven.[89]

We had followed the scriptural step-by-step process toward reconciliation, and Paul stated quite clearly that he desired to be treated as a "Gentile and a tax collector." In refusing to be reconciled Paul chose to remain bound to the sin.

When we forgive, each person is released from the bonds of sin; when we refuse to forgive, those who deny reconciliation deny Christ. Paul remains in his suffering, and rather than transforming his suffering by receiving Peter, who caused the harm yet was actively seeking reconciliation, Paul rejected him. In the process he rejected Christ. As priest for both, I pronounced God's absolution to the one penitent—Peter— and I continue to invite the unforgiving father—Paul—to be reconciled with God *and* his neighbor.

So what about Paul's gift? What happens when we continue to bring our tithes to church or serve Christ in other ways, without being reconciled with our neighbor?

> So when you are offering your gift at the altar, if you remember that your brother or sister has something against you, leave your gift there before the altar and go; first be reconciled to your brother or sister, and then come and offer your gift.[90]

The context is the Sermon on the Mount, in which Jesus reminds us what the life of blessing looks like and how we are to inhabit the way of the cross with each other. When I approach the altar of God, all the while refusing my neighbor as a gift from God, I suspend myself from friendship with God. The two go hand in hand. I do not keep the other from receiving Christ; rather, I am the one who suffers and keep myself from the forgiveness of Christ.

This is what it means to follow Christ, which is why G. K. Chesterton reminds us that, "The Christian ideal has not been tried and found

---

89. Matt. 18:15-19.
90. Matt. 5:21-24.

wanting. It has been found difficult; and left untried."[91] The faith of Christ calls us to inhabit our bodies more deeply. The primary demand it makes on us is that we love the Lord our God with all our heart, soul, mind, and strength.[92] And lest we separate this way of love from the actions of God in Christ, making love into something generic and altogether sentimental, Jesus reminds us that this means loving our neighbors as ourselves. This is the part that we find difficult; this is what we often leave untried.

It is also why we so readily speak of love and evade talk about Jesus and the cross. We want love somehow to be possible apart from pain and suffering. We want to wear tiny crosses around our necks, not carry heavy ones over our shoulders. But that's not the way of love. Love, like the birthing of a child, does not leave us unscathed; it is inseparable from the Person of Christ—the suffering of Christ. Jesus retains the nail scars and wound to the side even after his resurrection. And while the cross of Christ is an unrepeatable event in the history of the world it is an eternal event in the life of God, continually carrying us into being as we participate in its way—the way of humility. We hereby entrust ourselves to those who *can and cannot be trusted*, whereby trust is given before it is received. Again, the pattern is the cross. If we are to take seriously what it means to follow Christ as Savior and Lord we cannot proclaim any form of life that does not have the forgiveness of our enemies at its center.

---

91. G. K. Chesterton, *What's Wrong with the World* (San Francisco: Ignatius Press, 1994), 37.
92. Matt. 22:37; BCP, 324.

CHAPTER 15

Trusted into Trusting

As individuals we do not act; we exhibit behavior characteristic of the biological species and social group or groups to which we belong.

W. H. Auden

Walking in the way of peace, where we extend the peace of Christ even when we're not feeling so peaceful, takes practice. It is here that we must learn to trust the untrustworthy. My sister-in-law once visited us for a week in the summer as a brief getaway from the hustle and bustle of life. With four children under the age of eleven, life for her is often chaotic, and the time away afforded her the opportunity to catch up with Amanda, which does not come easy when children are always at your feet.

One night during Amy's visit, we played a game that our kids enjoy—*Settlers of Catan*. It's a game of strategy and tends to bring out one's competitive drive. With four players it tends to go quickly, but with five it seemed to take longer than expected. It was getting late, so we decided to leave the game on the table and finish it the next night. "Are we just going to leave it here?" Amy asked. "Yes," I responded. "Should we take a picture of the board in case anyone messes with it?" she inquired. "Nobody's going to mess with it," I said. To which Amanda added, "It will be fine. No one will touch anything." Reluctantly, Amy agreed to leave it as it was, although I suspect she wandered back and took a picture with her phone.

Amy has four young children who are always vying for power and attention. Her experience with people leaving things as they are has not been good, which inclined her not to trust the four of us to leave the game alone until we returned to it the next day. We live in a world of distrust. "If you see something, say something." Walk through any airport and you will hear repeated over and over again: "Please report any suspicious activity to the nearest TSA agent." Ever notice upon hearing these announcements how suspicious everyone around you starts to appear, especially if they seem to be from a Middle Eastern country? The announcement might as well say, "Trust no one!"

We work hard in our home to nurture a culture of trust. Even so, when the rest of the world is operating under the shadow of suspicion it can be difficult to sustain. Without realizing it, Amy was challenging our family's sense of trust, even though she, as the "outsider" in our environment, was the one least likely to be trusted. We are told not to entrust our luggage to another person, nor are we to carry someone else's belongings, and for good reason. Unbeknownst to Amy, she had carried into our home all the suspicious sensibilities of "civil" society.

We all do this. It's nearly impossible to avoid. Our sensibilities are affected and governed by a whole host of factors that move us in unsuspecting ways. Amy flew from Florida to New York to be with us, travelling through two airports, listening to the "suspicious activity warning" every three to five minutes. Amy's children would never trust their siblings to leave the game board alone overnight, a behavior she projected onto our children. It's understandable. Nevertheless, in the context of our home it is unreasonable.

Amanda and I have learned that we have to trust our children into becoming trustworthy. We have to trust them into trusting. They will not trust us if we do not trust them. They have betrayed and will, I'm sure, betray our trust again, but we have more to lose in not trusting them than we could ever gain otherwise. And at the end of the day, what do we have to lose? If one of our children moves a few pieces on a game board, what does it really matter? I might lose the game, but it's just a game. But what if the stakes are higher? What if the pieces on the board involve my job? If a coworker lies about what I've done or takes credit for my work, should I expose the liar? Should I become distraught and retaliate?

When I was in college I worked at a large bank in downtown Nashville, Tennessee. I was a personal banker, which is a glorified way of saying I opened bank accounts and helped people balance their checkbooks. Nevertheless, I had a modest amount of authority, just a little more than a teller. A bank teller who cashes and deposits your checks when you go to the bank has very limited power to cash a check, especially if it is not drawn on their particular bank. A person must have enough cash in their own bank account to cash a check that is not drawn on that bank. And any check over, say, $500 would need approval from a personal banker—me. My authority was only around $2,000. Anything above this threshold required the branch manager's approval.

Someone came into our branch one morning and wanted to cash a check for $10,000. Nobody does this—at least, it's highly unusual. People routinely cash their whole paycheck, even upwards of $2,000, but in the five years I was in and out of the banking industry I saw this happen once, and it was on this particular occasion. The teller immediately asked me to come over. I looked at the check, which was drawn on the U.S. Treasury, another red flag due to the difficulty of verifying the check's validity. I saw the amount and immediately said to the gentleman, "I'm sorry. This will require my manager's approval. She'll be back in an hour." On top of this, he didn't have an account with us. Another red flag.

I relayed the information to my manager when she returned and somewhat surprisingly the man returned an hour later with check in hand. He met with my manager who informed him that she would need to verify the check and he would need to return tomorrow. After he left, my manager said to me, "I am out of the office tomorrow in a managers' meeting downtown. If he comes back, call me and I'll let you know if it's approved or not." "Okay," I said.

The gentleman returned the next afternoon. As instructed, I called my manager during her meeting to ask if the check was approved to cash. She said that it was and to write her initials on the check. "Are you sure?" I asked. "Yes, it's fine," she replied. "Okay. Talk to you later." And I hung up the phone. The teller and I uneasily did as she requested, and the man walked out with $10,000 in cash.

The following Monday morning I arrived at work and someone from human resources was already meeting with my branch manager in her office. This wasn't unusual, but the manager was rarely there to open the bank otherwise. About thirty minutes into the workday she came out of her office and invited me to meet with the two of them. I walked in unsuspectingly. She shut the glass door behind her, sat down, and proceeded to inform me that the check *I* had approved last week was fraudulent and that *I* did not follow proper protocols and was being fired for not doing so. "*You* approved the check," I said. "I did not approve you to cash the check," she said without flinching. "Mike from human resources," she continued, "is going to do an exit interview with you and go over the details about why you're being let go." I was baffled. I've had people lie to me and about me, but never to the extent that it cost me my livelihood. I was young, newly married, and naïve enough to trust people to be moderately human.

Mike from human resources read her account of how things unfolded, how "I" approved the $10,000 check without her approval, and why this demanded my removal. He then asked, "Is there anything you would like to say in response?" "You mean," I began, "aside from everything that you just said being a lie? That I am being blamed for something I did not do? Do you mean anything besides me being wrongfully fired?" I asked. "If that's what you believe then you should write it down." Mike handed me a piece of paper with the accusation on it, which had room for a few lines of response. I wrote down a detailed account of what really happened and said to Mike, "So, am I really being fired for something I didn't do?" "It's not for me to say what you did or did not do, but you are being let go," Mike replied. Still in my confused state, I calmly said to Mike, "It seems to me that this is exactly what you're saying, and you should know that this makes you complicit."

I gathered my things from my desk, said goodbye to my coworkers, and walked over to my manager and calmly said, "I really don't understand why you would do this." To which she replied, "You need to leave the premises." I shook my head and walked out the door as calmly as possible.

When I came home and had to tell Amanda what had happened I could barely explain the situation. Had I been too trusting? Was I just young and naïve? Should I have made a fuss, perhaps gotten a lawyer involved? When Jesus sends the twelve disciples out to preach the Gospel, he says that he's sending them out like lambs in the midst of wolves, but that they are not to be wolves, even if they are to be wise and careful.[93] He tells the disciples to stay where they are welcomed and run when they're persecuted.[94] But he also tells them not to fret those who seek to hurt them.

> So have no fear of them; for nothing is covered up that will not be uncovered, and nothing secret that will not become known. Do not fear those who kill the body but cannot kill the soul; rather fear him who can destroy both soul and body in hell.[95]

Jesus seems to suggest that we need not concern ourselves with exposing the evil of others but that their evil will itself expose them. Darkness cannot hide from the light. We are also not to let the pain caused by another fester in us or determine our response. After all, the very worst a person can do is kill us. This sounds bad, but when we realize that death is not the worst thing that can happen to us we are on our way to life.

The bank branch closed soon thereafter and the manager lost her job. I took no delight in this. Instead, I found myself moved to pity. Maybe I shouldn't have felt sorry for her, but whatever pain or suffering had led her to injure me only brought about more suffering for her. I was but twenty-two. I found a job the next week. Nevertheless, my

---

93. Matt. 10.
94. Matt. 10:11, 23.
95. Matt. 10:26, 28.

experience on the other side of this event helped me to understand that following Christ is about living and loving in the confidence that whatever trial another person can bring upon me will always be temporary, and if I receive it with grace I will grow in faith—I will grow to trust God all the more, and my trust of God *in others* will not be scathed but strengthened, even when I am unjustly wronged.

This is where a faithful understanding of grace is of utmost importance. Our reluctance to forgive those who have wronged us stems from a misunderstanding of grace, which is conditioned, perhaps, by our frivolous practice of passing the Peace. We are right to believe that the person who harms us does not deserve forgiveness. No one who sins against us or does evil to another can ever deserve forgiveness. Indeed, there are none who deserve God's forgiveness; even the saintliest person we know does not deserve grace. This is the whole point of grace: *none* are deserving! And thanks be to God that we do not receive grace according to the measure of our deservedness. Recognizing grace as an absolute gift from God, given to all for the sake of our becoming worthy, opens us to own our mutual dependence on grace with sinner and saint alike.

This keeps us from setting ourselves and our personal virtues above those who struggle with sin and evil. It keeps me from thinking that my good is mine, for I know that only God is good.[96] When I locate the origin of my good actions in "me," failing to acknowledge that I can do no good apart from the goodness of God at work in me, this is when I lose all empathy, as well as any willingness to forgive. It is arrogance that leads me to believe that everyone has within them the power to do what is right and good. "If I can do it, they can do it." In arrogance we also deceive ourselves into believing our ability to do good originates with us. We deceive ourselves into believing that our good actions separate us from those who perform acts of sin and evil, as if there can be a good action that separates a person from others or elevates our status before God. Thomas Merton reminds us:

---

96. Luke 18:19.

As soon as you begin to take yourself seriously and imagine that your virtues are important because they are yours, you become the prisoner of your own vanity and even your best works will blind and deceive you. Then, in order to defend yourself, you will begin to see sins and faults everywhere in the actions of other men.[97]

When I consider the good that I do as my own good, rather than the goodness of God at work in me, the weaknesses of others become for me not an opportunity to extend the grace of which neither of us is deserving, but an occasion to feel better about myself. I come to believe that I am better than they. In the process, I succumb to my own self-deception, believing myself to be somehow superior or more loved by God. It is a sort of evolutionary theology, which falsely elevates the righteous as divinely selected, giving the strong in faith power to condemn the weak. Nothing could be further from the way of Christ. All have been selected for grace; and while none are deserving it is the responsibility of those who inhabit the way of Christ to draw out the grace of God at work in all people. When we do so, Christ is resurrected in our neighbors—Christ is resurrected in us, and God speaks to God in our midst. We enjoin ourselves to God's self-communication and come to participate one with another in the way of self-offering.

This is what it means to pass the Peace of Christ.

---

97. Merton, *New Seeds of Contemplation,* 58.

CHAPTER 16

Making Love Recognizable

The Lord's arm is not too short to save nor his ear too dull to hear;
rather, it is your iniquities that raise a barrier between you and your
God; it is your sins that veil his face, so that he does not hear.

Isaiah 59:1-2

Perhaps the most difficult aspect of this way of grace and peace is the many ways we anticipate another person's response. I *know* that the man with a gun is going to use it, so if I am to stop him I need to shoot first. I *know* that the person who stole from me will only do so again, so I remain guarded in his presence. What if our lack of faith—our lack of trust in God—is what moves others to turn away from grace? To put it differently, what if I attend solely to the grace of God at work in the world, at work in me, at work even in the worst of sinners? And what if my attentiveness to grace were the thing that chiefly conditions my disposition toward others? Could I alter another's tendency toward violence or evil if I am vulnerable to the Christ at work in our midst? Might my actions open them to behave according to the way of Christ, the way of love? Or, rather, could my *volitional participation* in grace alter another's imagination and reality, so as to move with grace and not against it?

Attending to grace in others is not always easy, especially if a person has given us cause for distrust. Nevertheless, it can be disabling for those who, having struggled with something in the past, attempt to regain the trust of family, friends, or a community. Jay is someone who found himself in exactly this situation. Jay was an alcoholic who found his way into our church one Sunday. Having grown up in a fundamentalist tradition, he was taken aback by the liturgy. As an accomplished pianist, he loved the hymnody and rhythm of the service. We spoke only briefly after the service. He conveyed his appreciation for the liturgy and went about his merry way. He showed up again the next week, and again the following. After his third visit, per my own custom, I invited him to have lunch with me so we could get to know each other. He agreed and we met later that week.

When he showed up for lunch on his bike in the middle of winter in western New York, I should have taken notice, but I didn't really think anything about it. We live in a college town and it is not unusual, even in winter, for someone to use a bike to travel short distances. Jay had lost his license due to a DUI, though there was no reason to suspect this initially. We started meeting regularly, as Jay was intrigued by our conversations and he always seemed to get the full meaning of my homilies on Sundays. Accustomed to having my preaching misinterpreted, I found it refreshing that Jay heard the whole thing!

After a few meetings it came up in conversation that Jay struggled with alcohol. "Oh," I said, "I guess I shouldn't have offered you that glass of wine the other day." "It's okay," he responded. "I don't really crave alcohol anymore and I don't like the way it makes me feel." That was the extent of our discussion on his life with alcohol. I never inquired further and he didn't feel the need to expound, although he would occasionally share with me things he was grateful to learn from his struggles, and how happy he was to know that he never hurt anyone in the process.

As I mentioned, Jay is an accomplished pianist, but due to his struggles he was forced to live in accommodations that were less conducive to sobriety. He managed well, but one of the setbacks was living with roommates and having no place to play the piano, so as to stay fresh. I told him that the church had great acoustics and a wonderful piano, and that he should consider using the space to practice. He was at first reluctant to accept my offer, but I told him he was welcome to use the space and to give me a call when he wanted to play. I informed him that I would let him in the first time, show him how to get in and turn the lights on, and that he could return anytime he wanted on his own.

Jay would eventually take me up on the offer to use the church to practice, and he expressed deep gratitude that I would trust him enough to give him access to the church. I looked at Jay and said rather plainly, "Jay, you're a part of our church now. This space is yours. It is for all of us to share and to offer our talents to God."

Jay continues to use the church to play, and he continues to show up for Sunday services. I could have seen Jay's history with alcohol as a red flag that he could not be trusted, but I believe in God, not Jay, and I trust the work that God has begun in Jay and the irresistible love of God to complete this work in him, so long as Jay has enough encouragement in Christ to himself become a volitive participant in grace. Jay has become worthy of trust, and while I cannot say whether he will ever betray my trust it is not for me to be concerned. My obligation as one who bears the name Christian is to trust God in Jay, and in everyone else, in the hope that they receive my trust as one receiving the grace of God.

My reason for trusting Jay—my reason for trusting anyone—has little to do with Jay. I trust Jay for the same reason that I trust anyone: I trust the God who is at work in the world, who is greater than any power or force of evil. I trust that when I attend to Christ in others that Christ himself is raised to the surface of their lives, and in the process each of us begins to see more clearly. Each of us becomes more and more worthy of trust, for it is the faith of Christ at work in us and in our midst.

I do not know if, had I become distrusting of Jay because of his history with alcohol, he would have become less trustworthy. That's not exactly how this works. Nor do I attribute his continued healing to my receptivity of him. What I do know, however, is that I can quickly become a stumbling block to anyone on their way to healing and grace if I doubt the sufficiency of God's grace to bring their lives to completion.[98] This is precisely what Paul is getting at when he tells the Corinthians that

---

98. 2 Cor. 12:9.

"Love is patient; love is kind. . . . It bears all things, believes all things, hopes all things, endures all things."[99] The way of love is the way of trust, trusting the untrustworthy into becoming trustworthy. Trusting those who have done wrong—those who have wronged us—and in a posture of vulnerability opening everyone we meet along the way to receive the forgiveness of Christ and thereby be received into his way of grace and peace—the way of love.

To follow in the way of incarnate love means recognizing that trust and distrust are relational. It is never just whether a person is trustworthy or untrustworthy. Trust and distrust are postures by which I receive others and others receive me. To be inhabited by grace is to remain ever open to others without closing others off through my own distrust.

---

99. 1 Cor. 13:4, 7.

Conclusion

I assure you that it is not by faith that you will come to know Christ, but by love; not by mere conviction but by action.

St. Gregory the Great

St. Augustine once said that we who are strong in faith must be careful not to trample all over God's meadow. If we do, says Augustine, "the weaker sheep will have to feed on trampled grass and drink from troubled waters."[100] We trample all over God's meadow when we refuse to trust Christ, trusting instead the misdeeds of those who struggle to live peaceably in this world. Instead of providing healing and nourishment to our weaker brothers and sisters we make it all the more difficult for them to pasture in God's meadow. When we receive others by grace—*with God's help*—we come to understand what it means to pass the Peace.

What if passing the Peace in our churches sounded more like, "I'm sorry," instead of, "Good morning"? What if we made time before approaching the altar of our Savior to make things right, to be reconciled with our neighbors, especially our neighbors in the adjoining pew? When the practice of passing the Peace is reduced to shaking hands and checking in with people we haven't seen since last Sunday, we gloss over

---

100. St. Augustine, "Sermon 47," in *Liturgy of the Hours* (Totowa: Catholic Book Publishing, 1986), 583.

the healing Christ makes available in the world. When we approach the one we have wronged or the one who wronged us, saying, "Things are not right between us and God. Let us be reconciled in Christ," we inhabit the peace of Christ, inviting the other to inhabit grace with us. To be reconciled is to invite others to be inhabited by the grace and forgiveness of *God with us*. When this becomes our ordinary practice in preparation for approaching the Lord's table we will know what reconciliation looks like. We will experience in our bodies the peace of Christ that passes all understanding.

In many of our churches, when the priest says, "The peace of the Lord be always with you," we respond, "And also with you." Something tells me that this is part of the problem. If we are attending to the Christ within each person, it seems to me that the better response is, "And with thy/your spirit." Why? It is not because there is division between the body and the spirit. Rather, when we say, "And with thy spirit," we become attentive to the truth of our bodies—the truth of our lives—as spirit. At the core of our being is Christ—Spirit. At the center of our lives is God—Spirit. When we respond to Christ in each other, we bear witness to the Spirit of God that enjoins us one to another, as we increase in awareness that right now, in the present moment of our life together in Christ, we inhabit the kingdom of God—life in the Spirit, worshiping God in spirit and in truth.

We acknowledge that we participate right now in the order of heaven. We confess that we are citizens not of this world but of God, and our heavenly citizenry in Christ makes claims on our life in the flesh. As in prayer, when we cry out to God saying, "Abba, Father," as Paul reminds, "it is that very Spirit bearing witness with our spirit that we are children of God."[101] Likewise, when we say, "And with thy spirit," God bears witness to God in our bearing witness to the God in each other, opening us to a union of spirits through our union in Christ's body. All of which is made possible through a posture of vulnerability.

---

101. Rom. 8:16.

Discussion Questions

1. Think about someone with whom you have been at odds. Have you been reconciled with this person? What is keeping you from making the first step? Or, if you've been reconciled, what fears did you have to overcome in order to seek forgiveness?

2. Why is it so easy for us to see what others do wrong? How might this impact our ability or willingness to seek forgiveness, especially if we are the one who was wronged?

3. Think of a time when you have experienced real suffering. How has this helped you become more empathic toward others? Has it enabled you to be more forgiving toward those who disagree with you or who have hurt you in some way?

PART IV

The Heavenly Banquet

"This is My Body"

Therefore I tell you, do not worry about your life, what you will eat or what you will drink, or about your body, what you will wear. Is not life more than food, and the body more than clothing? Look at the birds of the air; they neither sow nor reap nor gather into barns, and yet your heavenly Father feeds them. Are you not of more value than they? And can any of you by worrying add a single hour to your span of life? And why do you worry about clothing? Consider the lilies of the field, how they grow; they neither toil nor spin, yet I tell you, even Solomon in all his glory was not clothed like one of these. But if God so clothes the grass of the field, which is alive today and tomorrow is thrown into the oven, will he not much more clothe you—you of little faith? Therefore do not worry, saying, "What will we eat?" or "What will we drink?" or "What will we wear?" For it is the Gentiles who strive for all these things; and indeed your heavenly Father knows that you need all these things. But strive first for the kingdom of God and his righteousness, and all these things will be given to you as well. So do not worry about tomorrow, for tomorrow will bring worries of its own. Today's trouble is enough for today.

Matthew 6:25-34

CHAPTER 17

Turn Toward Christ

Our eyes are not in focus for God's reality, until they are out of focus for our own petty concerns.

Evelyn Underhill

'm next to the priest," she said as she made her way into the seat adjacent to mine on the plane. I was seated in the middle between two older women, one meek and mild and the other somewhat abrasive. I smiled as she climbed into her seat and I realized that this leg of the flight was not going to be as uneventful as my previous one connecting to Atlanta. On that flight I was seated next to a gentleman, slightly older than me, who bent over backward to make me feel comfortable. He put up and took down my luggage in the rack above, shared his snacks with me, took care of my trash, yet spoke very few words. The woman to my left on my flight to Daytona, however, made it clear that she was somewhat anxious to sit next to "the priest."

I wear my clericals most everywhere I go, especially when I'm travelling. I do this because I can't help but think how strange it is for priests to go about incognito in the world. I am not in the majority on this issue, but I do think I'm right. I remember one priest who told me that he doesn't need to wear his collar for people to know he is a priest. "This is true," I said, "but neither do I speak with every person who can see me walking down the street. But when they see a priest doing ordinary things," I said, "I think it helps them remember that God is present in the ordinary." Besides, it's really me that needs to be reminded that I'm a priest. Not anyone else.

As she buckled herself into the seat next to mine, Rachel asked, "Are you Roman Catholic?" "No," I said, "I'm an Episcopal priest." "But you're a priest?" she asked. "Yes," I said. "I'm Catholic," she went on. "I've been in Rochester for a funeral—a big Catholic funeral, very churchy," she explained. "I'm a religious person," she offered, showing me a Malcolm Gladwell book that she was reading. I'm still not sure how reading Malcolm Gladwell makes one religious, unless she reads him religiously. I was amused by her felt need to confess to this priest how religious she was, as if I cared. Rachel went on to say that, "God and me, we have an understanding. He takes care of me. He doesn't need me to go to church every Sunday." "You're right," I said. "What?" she responded, seemingly surprised by my agreement with her. "You're right," I reiterated, "God doesn't need you." And with that, Rachel had nothing else to say to me.

Rachel did something I've heard many people do in my presence. Before I knew better, I often thought people were trying to convince me that they and God had a good relationship and that everything is okay in their lives, but what I realized more clearly than ever with Rachel is that she wasn't trying to convince *me* of anything. Rather, Rachel was trying to convince herself that she was okay—that she and God are okay.

It is always fascinating how "religious" some people become when they are in the presence of clergy. I much prefer those who keep on smoking and swearing when I wander by, though I admit it is comical when people attempt to hide their cigarettes when I happen upon them. As if I care—as if God cares, or as if the smell magically vanishes when the cigarette is tucked behind their backs. Such persons hide their habits because they feel as though smoking and God don't go together. They seem to think that God abhors "curse words." Smoking is not healthy; this is not a secret. But is it worse than overeating? Is it worse than drinking too much? Is it worse than owning two homes? Is it worse than spending five to ten dollars a day on lattes? Is it worse than the hours we spend caressing our cell phones? (The American average is about three hours a day.) The judgments we make are our own self-condemnations. The real question we are avoiding is whether our habits are turning us toward or away from Christ. What do my habits turn me to?

In his little-known book *Act and Being,* Dietrich Bonhoeffer writes that "being in Christ is being *turned to* Christ, and this is possible only through 'being already' in the communion of Christ."[102] We exist, says Bonhoeffer, by virtue of our being created in the image of God, as part of God's own life. Therefore, when we "find God" or "discover Christ" it is not because God was lost or Christ was playing hide-and-go-seek; rather, we come into contact with our true selves. Turning toward Christ through the habits of faith turns us to the truth of who we are as icons of Christ. We are already "in the communion of Christ."[103] To know who we are, however, requires what the earliest Christians called *askesis,* a life of discipline. It requires contact with God through habits of faith.

I wonder if we might think through this life of discipline with a saint who struggled with discipline. St. Augustine, who once prayed, "O Lord, make me chaste, but not yet," actually goes on to create a monastic order within the church governed by harsh discipline—*askesis*—but eventually leaves the order because he finds it too difficult. I don't know about you, but Augustine is my kind of saint. How often have we created a workout routine or diet, only to adjust it all along the way to make it easier, and in the end echoing comedian Jim Gaffigan after the first day of our workout: "Well, I didn't mean I'd work out *every* day."[104]

---

102. Dietrich Bonhoeffer, *Act and Being* (New York: Harper & Brothers Publishers, 1961), 177, italics mine.

103. When Bonhoeffer refers to the "communion of Christ," he refers distinctly to the body of Christ—the church. I would not exclude, as Bonhoeffer might, non-Christians from communion with Christ, in the specific sense that all live and move and have their being in God. Our awareness of this reality, however, I would suggest requires participation in the movement of the church with Christ's agency in the world.

104. *Jim Gaffigan: Mr. Universe,* perf. Jim Gaffigan, Washington, DC, April 11, 2012, accessed August 7, 2018.

To turn toward Christ is a matter of changing our minds. The Greek word μετεμελήθητε (*metameletheta*),[105] which we translate as "to change your mind," is not just a simple call to *think* differently; rather, it is to turn our thoughts in a different direction by turning our bodies toward something else—by turning our habits toward Christ.[106] It's the same sort of turning that an alcoholic might make by entering rehab, in order to turn himself away from the lure of alcohol. Anyone who has tried to remove a bad habit has learned that you cannot so much remove a habit as replace it. Something new must replace the old, or else the old habit will return, often with a vengeance. Turning toward Christ, therefore, is not a simple matter of turning away from things that are bad for us; it is a tangible turning of our hearts *to* Christ. This involves a re-habituation of desire, whereby our senses attend not to what is passing and fleeting, but to the deep longing for Christ that lies at the core of our humanity.

So what does this look like? Let me offer an example from my home. Our dining table is an old farm table, once used in a boarding school dining hall. It had been sitting in storage collecting dust and mildew for years, following the building of a new refectory on campus. There were initials carved into the table from students gone before. The stain was beginning to peel and scratch. And there were rough patches on either end due to water damage. I was given one of these tables to use in our home. We cleaned it, but we did not at first do any work on the table. It was quite sturdy; only the surface needed to be manicured.

One afternoon my daughter and I took the table, sanded it down, wiped it clean, and lo and behold this 150-year-old table, as sturdy as ever, looked pristine. It retained the character of student initials and small cracks from old age, but it was otherwise restored to its original

---

105. In addition to *metameletheta*, the other word used for "change your mind" in the New Testament is *metanoia*, which means to repent—quite literally "to turn around."
106. See Matt. 21:32. Jesus describes this "changing of the mind" with the parable of the two sons whose father asked them to go work in the vineyard. The first son said he would and didn't; the second said he wouldn't, but "changed his mind" and went to work in the field. The Pharisees refused to change their minds about how they carried out the Law after John called them to repentance. This change of mind is inseparable from the change of practice—a change of heart.

glory. Time and poor storage conditions had rendered the table filthy and unusable. Nevertheless, once the grime and decay were stripped away, what rose to the surface was a beautiful table that now makes dining a pleasure. This table has seen numerous meals, entertained countless guests, and helped complete innumerable homework projects and assignments. It has been a place of joy and sorrow, a place of laughter and many tears. And it is a prayerful table, praying for meals with our family and routinely joining in the Lord's Prayer with us before bed. Once it was in storage without a family or purpose; now it resides in our kitchen, gathering our family and many friends together each and every day. Having shed its outer nature of grime and decay, the table's true nature as a place of gathering and hospitality has risen to the surface, making our home likewise a place of gathering and hospitality.

In the seventh century, Maximus Confessor offered a new conception of a word held dear by the earliest Christians seeking to follow the narrow way of Christ. *Apatheia*, from which we get *apathy*, bears a meaning well beyond our colloquial "lack of interest." We often think of *apathy* as the opposite of *empathy*, as in, "My son is apathetic toward doing his homework." While this may account for its modern usage outside of certain philosophical circles, it hides the rich meaning shared by early followers of Christ. Even more recent attempts to offer a sympathetic rendering of *apatheia* often reduce its meaning to a "state of mind." *Apatheia,* however, has to do with the passions, in the specific sense of human desire.

Philosophers speak of appetites, namely the appetites of the soul, not just our cravings at the dinner table. The philosopher Aristotle goes so far as to include appetites in his description of the soul, which consists of the intellective and the appetitive, eerily similar to right- and left-brain functions. Maximus and other Christian theologians continued to work with this definition of the soul, reaching well beyond philosophy in an attempt to account for the hidden realities of human passions. Maximus describes this dynamic as a "secret disposition."[107] Thomas Aquinas calls

---

107. Maximus Confessor, "Chapters on Love," in *Maximus Confessor: Selected Writings*, trans. George C. Berthold (New York: Paulist Press, 1985), III.69; see also "Letter 2."

it a "natural appetite."[108] Each refers to an understanding of human desire by which we align our bodies with our true nature—our *natural nature*—hidden in Christ.

For Maximus, the passions are not simply negative, as theologians before and after him are prone to describe them. The passions are typically understood to be those unruly desires of fallen human nature—licentiousness, gluttony, and the like. But Maximus describes something different. By locating true human desire in the soul, which preexists in the eternal *Logos*—Christ—Maximus refuses to define passion as something that *only* leads one away from the love of God in Christ. "A blameworthy passion," he writes, "is a movement of the soul contrary to nature."[109] Yet *pathos*—human passion and desire—rightly ordered, elicits from us the true nature of the soul—our "natural nature."[110] *Apatheia* for Maximus is not a simple suppression of desire; it is not the Stoic elimination of human passion toward a particular state of mind; rather, *apatheia* describes a shedding away of false passions and desires in order for the principle (*logoi*)[111] of one's being to rise to the surface, so that we might move *naturally* toward God.

As with the refectory table that was stored in a damp basement, where [mold] and [dust] consume,[112] misaligned passions have a way of keeping our souls in hiding. They keep our true passion for God and our natural love for our neighbors from orienting us to God and opening us to the hospitality of Christ. The unnatural passions that cover over our *natural nature* lead only to decay. However, our natural passions, which rise to the surface of our lives when we attend to Christ, increase in us

---

108. Aquinas, *Summa Theologica,* vol. I (Allen: Christian Classics, 1981), I.I.80.
109. Maximus, "Chapters on Love," I.35.
110. Maximus, "Ambiguum 7," 1084D, p. 107.
111. For Maximus, the eternal Logos holds within the *logoi* of all creation, including humans. Humans are, therefore, portions of God. This is the way in which Maximus describes what it means to be created in the image of God. When we are attentive to our *natural nature* as a *logoi* of the *Logos,* it is then that we learn to desire the things of God. See "Ambiguum 7."
112. Please forgive my play on words here with Matt. 6:19.

the hospitality of Christ, proportionate to our love and care for others. *As we move with Christ, so we come to desire the things of God.*

This is the same dynamic that James articulates in his epistle. In James 4, he speaks of passion as something *at war* within us.

> Those conflicts and disputes among you, where do they come from? Do they not come from your cravings that are at war within you? You want something and do not have it; so you commit murder. And you covet something and cannot obtain it; so you engage in disputes and conflicts. You do not have, because you do not ask. You ask and do not receive, because you ask wrongly, in order to spend what you get on your pleasures.[113]

In speaking of these "cravings," James uses the Greek word ἐπιθυμεῖτε (*epithumeite*), meaning "to turn toward." The passions of the body have to do with our attention. They have to do with what or who we are facing—what or who we are *turned toward*. Aligning our passions to Christ is a matter of aligning our bodies in accordance with the rhythm of holiness.

Attention to the Christ in all things—*turning toward* Christ in all people, places, and things, even in a worn-out old farm table—brings a newness of life that cannot at first be anticipated or fully imagined. This is *apatheia*. It is the shedding of false passions that keep us from the love of God in Christ, so that our true passion—our true desire, which is our longing for God—will draw our hearts, guide our minds, fill our imaginations, and control our wills, turning us toward Christ to be used by God for his glory and for the benefit of all others.[114] As Rowan Williams helpfully clarifies, this understanding of the emotional life is not about suppressing our emotions or someone doing away with them so that we become apathetic. Rather, it "is about the rational inhabiting and understanding of the instinctual life in such a way that it doesn't take over and dictate your relations with God or with one another."[115]

---

113. James 4:1-3.
114. See "A Prayer of Self-Dedication" in BCP, 832.
115. Rowan Williams, *Holy Living*, 119.

This is a far cry from "apathy." It is a deep longing for Christ, having our senses completely charged by incarnate love in such a way that we forsake all false gods—all false ways of loving. For, as in a good marriage, when we forsake all others and turn our bodies completely toward one person, it is then that we know best how to love others. I can embrace others in love because I know what it means to embrace my wife. I can faithfully relate to all others without reducing any to an object of desire when my desire for the peculiar form of marital intimacy is turned toward one person. In like manner, it is my *turning toward* Christ, my longing to be at one with God, that frees me from the selfishness of bodily passions that might incline me to use another for my own benefit. Being turned toward God and ready to be used by God for his glory and to the benefit of all others saves me from using others for my own benefit or my own glory. Yet if the passions that govern my life are not the true passion of the soul for God, then my desire will always be offline, as it were; it will be unable to connect with the depths of my true nature. Unable to connect with my true self, hidden in Christ, I will find myself continually striving for a self that does not exist.

Selfishness, at the end of the day, is the attempt to satiate the desires of a self that does not accord with our true nature. And because this self does not actually exist there can be no *end* to its desire. It is insatiable. Everything it consumes throws me into an abyss, suspending peace and contentment. When our desire is singularly for God, however, peace and contentment are a natural occurrence because the peace of loving God accords with our *natural nature*. To turn toward God is to be turned toward our true selves as an image of God. The end of humans is God; when our desire is for God our passions are aligned. And although our desire for God is never-ending, it nonetheless brings peace and contentment because it accords with our natural desire; it accords with our true selves as humans—as *imago Dei*.

CHAPTER 18

The "Amen!" Heard 'Round the World

The Eucharist is the sacrament of cosmic remembrance: it is indeed a restoration of love as the very life of the world.

Alexander Schmemann

We have already discussed the postures of the body that make this turning toward Christ possible, and it is crucial for us to own the reality that our bodily awareness is how our souls rise to govern the life of faith. In Christianity, there is no division between the body and soul. What we do with our bodies conditions how we relate to God and others, and the principle way that Christians turn their bodies toward Christ is in the Eucharist.

I experience this turning routinely as one who presides over Eucharistic celebrations every week. Nevertheless, if we are not careful there are aspects of prayer and liturgy that we can easily de-emphasize by our familiarity with them, which often happens with us unaware. This is why altering our liturgies with the seasons and experiencing liturgy in other places are vital practices. Worshiping in another tradition or church can renew our own participation in the movement of worship at home, which may strike us in unexpected and wonderfully jarring ways.

Our family had the rare opportunity to visit another church when we were living in Maryland. As a priest, having a free Sunday either means that I am away for continuing education or on a family vacation. I was a chaplain at the time, which meant that school breaks often equaled a break from leading worship. A friend of mine was the priest at St. Paul's in Sharpsburg, Maryland, a small, country church near the Antietam battlefield. Sharpsburg is known for two things: the Battle of Antietam (known as the day when more Americans died in battle than on any other day in American history) and Nutter's Ice Cream (the best and cheapest ice cream that side of the Mason-Dixon line). Not a thriving metropolis, Sharpsburg sits at the border of West Virginia and Maryland, surrounded by cornfields. Nevertheless, because of its location it tends to have a fair number of cyclists passing through, as the roads around Antietam are scenic and good for training. On this particular Sunday when our family was visiting St. Paul's, during the homily a young man in blue spandex and plastic cyclist shoes clamored into the pew behind us. It was not unusual for cyclists to drop in for church, as I would eventually learn; nevertheless, this man was an unusual cyclist. He had long blond hair, a somewhat protruding nose, and was lanky, noisy, and, again, blue from head to toe.

Our children were eight and ten at the time, and our daughter found the blue cyclist quite entertaining. Her giggling only seemed to accentuate his continual hair flips and squirming in the creaky pew behind us. The service continued with the Eucharistic Prayer as normal, and we regained composure, with modest resistance from our children. The young man was obviously an Episcopalian, as he participated with ease throughout the service. But his sensibilities were seemingly a far cry from the typical, reserved Episcopalian. This fact was made abundantly clear to every farmer in the room when, at the final elevation where the celebrant says, "By whom and with whom and in whom, in the unity of the Holy Spirit, all honor and glory are yours, O Father Almighty, world without end," the blue, Episcopal cyclist blurted out the "Amen!" heard 'round the world. I felt the pew shake behind me as one farmer after another in front of us turned to see whence the sound had come. It was quite a moment, to say the least.

The "Amen" at the elevation, known as the "Great Amen," has become less great over the years, attended with a more somber tone. To highlight its importance, however, the Great Amen is printed in all caps, which is a shift from the 1928 prayer book, intended to highlight the culmination of the Eucharistic Prayer and the crescendo, as it were, of the Spirit's descent upon the Eucharistic elements *and* the people there gathered. Naturally, this is a joyous moment. God in Christ, through the power of the Holy Spirit, descends upon the church. This is good news! This is a truth worthy of all to be received. It is worth shouting about, crying out to God, saying, "Yes, this is true!" "Amen!"

The cry from the pew behind us was a reminder to this priest that it is easy to forget just how mysterious and life changing the body and blood of Christ truly is. What I realized in that moment, however, is the connection between our vocalized "Amen" and what we understand to be taking place before our very eyes. A whispered "Amen" may not bear witness to the God who has come down from heaven. A breathless "Amen" does not bespeak the mystery of God made man, born of a Virgin, dead, buried, and resurrected, who has ascended into heaven and will come again to restore us to our *natural nature*. Not only this, the somberness with which we often utter this word has reconditioned our sensibilities to think of this meal as some sort of symbolic ritual. I don't know about you, but I'm with Flannery O'Connor on this one: "If it's just a symbol, then to hell with it."

Now, I'm not sure the solution to heighten our awareness of this mystery is to suddenly have everyone start yelling from the top of their lungs, "Amen!" Yet we must own the connection between what we believe to be happening in, by, and through this bread and wine and the manner of our "Amen."

We who live in the modern world are prone to domestication. We are prone to keep things under control and in line. When communities face problems or difficulties, we write laws instead of confronting or, dare I say, getting to know our neighbors. When our children do something good or when they get out of line we implement rewards and punishments, rather than expressing joyful love or loving concern. As we have learned from neuroscience, when a situation catches our attention and we feel out of control, we often shift into "left-hemisphere" brain mode and begin problem-solving. Instead of opening ourselves to the human condition and experience underway (right-hemisphere mode), we become fixers.[116] In the process we lose the bigger picture. We lose mystery, vulnerability, empathy, and more as we try to fix the person or thing to suit our domesticated sensibilities.[117] If we are going to be transformed by the incarnate mystery of feasting on Christ's body and blood our practices must attend to the life-changing grace set before us. In other words, with complete attention to Christ in the Eucharist we must rejoice in his being present with us and fervently declare: "AMEN!"

---

116. Ian McGilchrist, *The Master and his Emissary* (New Haven: Yale University Press, 2009), 65.
117. Ibid., 32-93.

CHAPTER 19

Bread from Heaven

All animals eat. An animal that eats and thinks must think big about what it is eating not to be taken for an animal.

Adam Gopnik

I gazed upon the lovely face of Christ," says Charles Williams, "and the dove of peace alighted upon me. I gazed upon the dove of peace and it flew away."[118] Williams names our tendency to get distracted by the benefits of Christ's presence. When we gaze upon Christ and order our life by the presence of God in our midst, peace does come, even amidst the "flying loves and fading lusts" of this world,[119] as G. K. Chesterton puts it. Yet when we focus on the peace that comes and turn our gaze away from Christ and the Way of Love in the world, it becomes all too fragile; it flies away.

Our kids have received Eucharist since they were infants, as I am a firm believer in not stopping children from approaching Christ. One Sunday Wyles, at the time four years old, knelt beside me at the altar rail as priests and chalice bearers distributed the Eucharistic food. The priest

---

118. A friend, now deceased, once shared this quote with me.
119. G. K. Chesterton, "The Great Minimum," in *The Collected Poems of G. K. Chesterton* (London: Methuen, 1933), 132-133.

came to me, placed the host in my hand, and repeated those familiar words, "The body of Christ, the bread of heaven." The priest proceeded to give Communion to Wyles. He extended his palms in the shape of a cross and the priest uttered those familiar words once more. Wyles took the host into his fingers and, putting it in front of my face, he asked me, "Is this *really* bread from heaven?" Fending off tears of joy, I looked at Wyles and said, "Yes, it is bread from heaven." Wyles smiled, as he placed the body of Christ into his mouth with complete confidence that he was feasting on the bread of gods.

We can grow too familiar with this bread. Week after week the heavenly wafer is placed in the palm of our hands, and we all too nonchalantly ingest something that often struggles to resemble bread, much less convey nourishment from heaven. And as we turn our gaze upon the pseudo-bread we often fail to see Christ. We trust our eyes and taste buds too much, failing to hear the truth of *God with us*.

Thomas Aquinas is known for his supreme intellect, but he was also quite the poet, a wonderful liturgist, not to mention the writer of my favorite hymns. In one of his prayers, which he would often pray at the elevation of the Eucharist, Aquinas writes:

> Devoutly I adore You, hidden Deity, / Under these appearances concealed. / To You my heart surrenders self / For, seeing You, all else must yield. / Sight and touch and taste here fail; / Hearing only can be believed. / I trust what God's own Son has said. / Truth from truth is best received.[120]

As Aquinas rightly notes, if we trust what we see with our eyes or taste in our mouths, our senses will betray us. However, if we stop and ask ourselves, "Is this *really* bread from heaven?" and we turn our eyes and taste buds toward the truth of Christ who, by the power of the Holy Spirit, came down from heaven, we can recognize Christ in the sacrament. This does not, however, mean that we ignore what we see and taste in the

---

120. Thomas Aquinas, "Adoro Te Devote, Latens Deitas" in *The Aquinas Prayer Book* (Manchester: Sophia Institute Press, 2000), 69.

Eucharist; rather, it means that we learn to trust not simply what we see and taste but we grow to savor God in this morsel of bread and wine that has come down from heaven.

It is a matter of *sapientia*. *Sapientia* is the Latin word for wisdom. However, this word-for-word translation betrays the fullness of what wisdom really is. *Sapientia* is intimately connected with *sapor,* or *savor*. Wisdom and taste are inseparable. Wisdom, we might say, is a disciplined hunger for true knowledge. For our purposes, wisdom is a palate that has learned to savor God in the Eucharist, trusting the wisdom that has come from above to taste and see God.

Acquiring taste takes time and always involves adjustments to our sensibilities. This can be off-putting, even unpleasant, especially after failed attempts, whether we're searching for God or trying a new recipe. My first glass of wine, for instance, was terrible. I truly wondered why anyone drank the stuff. I had been waiting tables at Brentwood Country Club in Brentwood, Tennessee. One of the perks of working there was being fed at every shift. Being a college student, I was thrilled to have food I neither cooked nor paid for. In addition, a couple times a year the country club would have a party for the service staff. They would close one of the banquet rooms, put down a dance floor, hire a DJ, and prepare modestly better food than the typical fare. The food was nothing special, but, again, it was a meal that cost me nothing in either money or effort. So I went. I discovered that the music was loud, the food was indeed mediocre, and the drinks consisted of domestic beer and cheap wine. Being twenty at the time, and having grown up in a fairly conservative home, I had only had one beer at that point in my life. Upon learning this, one of my coworkers made it her objective to find something I would enjoy. When I took my first sip of cheap wine, my mouth did this thing it had never done before. It twisted and contorted, and my eyes crumpled, as if staring into the sun.

It would be some time before I attempted another sip of wine, and only then after consulting a sommelier. My palate was not ready. It may have been the wine; it may have been the sensitivity of my taste buds. Whatever the case may be, wine and I did not agree.

This is analogous to life with Christ. It is why Paul says he fed the Corinthians with milk, not solid food.[121] Paul tells them that they are not ready for solid food; their palates are not yet ready for wine. Why? The Corinthians had not yet begun to order their lives by the *sapientia* of God. What they saw and tasted still governed how they interpreted life in Christ.

To know Christ is to learn how to savor Christ in ordinary food; it is also a matter of becoming the flavor of God in the world—salt that doesn't lose its saltiness,[122] so that we see Christ in others and all people begin to see Christ in us, in others, and the active agency of God in the world. Wisdom is a matter of re-habituating our sensibilities to the truth of *God with us*. In the final section, we will discuss how to do this in a way that is sustainable as practitioners of faith. For now, it is important to linger here for a moment and recognize how easily we allow our senses to be governed by food that turns us away from Christ.

---

121. 1 Cor. 3:2.
122. Matt. 5:13.

CHAPTER 20

Discerning the Body

For the fully Christian life is a Eucharistic life: that is, a natural life conformed to the pattern of Jesus, given in its wholeness to God, laid on His altar as a sacrifice of love, and consecrated, transformed by His inpouring life, to be used to give life and food to other souls.

Evelyn Underhill

In his letter to the Corinthians, Paul tells the people that if they do not discern the body of Christ, they eat and drink judgment instead of life.

Examine yourselves, and only then eat of the bread and drink of the cup. For all who eat and drink without discerning the body, eat and drink judgment against themselves. For this reason many of you are weak and ill, and some have died. *But if we judged ourselves, we would not be judged.* But when we are judged by the Lord, we are disciplined so that we may not be condemned along with the world. So then, my brothers and sisters, when you come together to eat, wait for one another. If you are hungry, eat at home, so that when you come together, it will not be for your condemnation.[123]

---

123. 1 Cor. 11:28-34, italics mine.

It is hard to imagine anyone in our churches bringing food to a potluck and, while everyone else is getting their food from the common table, placing it on their own table for themselves and inviting only their closest friends to eat their food with them. Yet this is the scene that Paul describes. The Corinthians were gathering for a shared meal as the body of Christ; however, they retained all the societal class divisions, refusing to pass the food around for all to partake. They only broke bread with people of their own class. Even the worst of sinners would not attempt this today. Nevertheless, the ease with which we separate ourselves based on politics, gender, race, and religion is often appalling. It may not involve food and it may not even involve class, but we nonetheless become our own judge when we turn our gaze upon the problem at hand instead of the Christ in each. When Paul says that the Corinthians are not ready for solid food, he is suggesting that if they can't even recognize the food they buy in the market as something to be shared, how are they ever going to perceive Christ in the Eucharist? How are they ever going to love their neighbors as themselves? How could anyone possibly expect to receive God if they cannot even receive the stranger?

The sacramental body of Christ is inseparable from how we relate to each other. If we gather as a church and are segregated by income, class, education, race, gender, or any other worldly division it is safe to say that we are *not* discerning the body of Christ. Paul suggests that when we fix our gaze only upon those who are like us, our gaze is not on Christ. We only see bread; we do not see heaven. Jesus puts it this way: "If you only love and care for those who love and care for you, you're no better than any other sinner."[124] To see Christ in the Eucharistic feast is to see Christ in each other, and if we do not see Christ in each other we will hardly recognize the Eucharist to be heavenly food. And yet this dynamic remains an obstacle for many of our churches.

This struggle to see more than is at first present to the eyes is not an individual struggle. It is symptomatic of much broader cultural influences. What has increasingly come to govern human sensibilities in the

---

124. Luke 6:31-36.

modern world is the notion of autonomy. Ironically, this runs parallel with the increasing connectedness we are experiencing relative to communication technologies and platforms. It is also interesting to note that the more our tools mediate our relationships the less empathic we become, even toward family and friends.[125] Arguably, these "connectors" are disconnecting us more and more; nevertheless, it is increasingly difficult to claim autonomy. Yet as René Girard has noted, "People do not want to be told that they are not autonomous. . . ."[126] We like to think that we are the choosers of our own destinies—that we make our world. But what if our sensibilities, and therefore everything we perceive or imagine to be true, are conditioned largely by imperceptible forces working on us from the outside? And what if these same forces are continually throwing us into being, altering our relationships, educating our temperaments, and disciplining our relationship with God? The reason, says René Girard, that people do not want to hear that they are not autonomous is because they do not want to believe that "others are acting through them."[127]

As we saw in part 2, everything affects how we make our way in the world. Yet we are not merely puppets on a stage. We do act. We do show up for things. Nevertheless, before we act—before we do anything—we are related. We are first and foremost dependent, contingent on external and even internal forces over which we have minimal control. I don't get to decide, for instance, what the weather is like today. If it's raining, however, I can decide to use an umbrella or enjoy getting wet. When a person is walking by me on the sidewalk gazing down and avoiding eye contact (as so often happens in the college town where I live), I can ignore the person or I can break the apparent awkwardness of our proximity by saying, "Good morning!" In one version of the situation I allow society's fear of the stranger to govern my sensibilities, thereby restraining myself from greeting the person on the sidewalk. In the other, I give myself to the hospitality of Christ who knows no stranger, and I offer a simple

---

125. McGilchrist, *The Master and his Emissary,* 111-115, 439.

126. René Girard, *Battling to the End* (East Lansing: Michigan State University Press, 2010), 72.

127. Ibid.

"Good morning!" This greeting reminds the other person and me that though we may not know one another we are nonetheless related.

Modern society has unfortunately taught us that our natural relatedness is unnatural. We have learned to see our disagreements and differences not as opportunities to expand our horizons, but as obstacles to be overcome, confronted, or removed.

CHAPTER 21

Sense-Perplexity
and Divine *Terroir*

The intellect that is not fertilized by imagination guided by the heart is sterile.

Meditations on the Tarot

What I am more and more convinced keeps us from the full stature of Christ is a lack of curiosity. We lack a sense of wonder toward God, the world, and each other. One of my favorite prayers in the prayer book is the final prayer at Holy Baptism. We give thanks to God for the gift of water and for inhabiting the baptized with the new life of grace, and then we ask God to "Give them an inquiring and discerning heart, the courage to will and to persevere, a spirit to know and to love you, *and the gift of joy and wonder in all your works.*"[128]

The great philosopher Socrates says that "wonder is the feeling of a philosopher, and philosophy begins in wonder."[129] In a dialogue with Theaetetus, Socrates begins to speak of those he refers to as the "uninitiated." The uninitiated are those who believe in what they "grasp in their

128. BCP, 308, italics mine.
129. Plato, *The Theaetetus*, trans. M. J. Levett (Indianapolis: Hackett Publishing, 2002), 173e-174b, 301-302.

hands." Amidst the dialogue recounted by Plato between Socrates and
Theaetetus, we hear Socrates describing wonder as a kind of human virtue, whereby our curiosity about a hidden energy or motion enables us
to see with, yet beyond, whatever material lies before us. This "feeling"
of wonder is what Socrates describes as a kind of *sense-perplexity*. That
is, rather than stopping at what we experience through our senses, we try
to understand the hidden dimension of the energy that has aroused our
senses. In the experience of happiness, for instance, we either stop at the
taste and sensation of a glass of fine wine, or we give attention to the *gout
de terroir—the taste of a place*.

Terroir in French has to do specifically with winemaking, yet in a
deeply cultural sense. The *gout de terroir* names the deep connection
between the soil, the hands that tend the vines, the quality of the grape,
and the sensory delight of the wine. In other words, the wine—its fullness of taste and heightening of our senses—cannot be separated from
any of the environmental circumstances and people within which and
by whom it is produced. The *gout de terroir* is irreducible to individual
taste; it names the heart of a culture, a way of life where vine, vine-
grower, and vino-producer are inseparable. For this reason, it is actually
illegal to label a wine with the name Bordeaux if it is not from Bordeaux,
France. (A South African wine has had some fun with this labeling
restriction, naming their Bordeaux-like wine "Bored-Doe.") Bordeaux
is at once the wine and the place; the two are inseparable. When I drink
a glass of Bordeaux from Bordeaux, France, I am ingesting more than
a glass of wine; I am taking into my soul a place, a culture—*a pattern
of life*.

To be curiously perplexed requires habits of wonder, remaining
ever open to being mystified by the ordinary. It is a *sapiential* knowing, whereby our contact with the things of God give way to wonder,
rather than merely taking something for granted. In the foyer of our
house there is a picture with a statement that has become something of a
catchphrase, but it suits the lives of those who inhabit our home: "Not all
who wander are lost." I have come to believe that wonder and wander,
separated in the English language only by a single vowel, have far more
in common than just five other letters.

In Plato's *Theaetetus*, "perplexity" is what leads to wonder. When we are perplexed by something, our minds wander. We begin to ponder things anew and reconsider preconceived ideas about a person, place, or thing. We wonder about these in such a way that we become open. We are opened to a new experience of what has caused us to be perplexed. When I turn my imagination toward the mysterious embodiment, the mysterious presence of Christ in creation, trees become irreducible to air-purifying plants that filter the toxins of the world so I can breathe better. They are not other than this, but they are so much more. I begin to see in each and every tree an energy that precedes a particular tree and yet proceeds from all trees, inclining me to see how the mystery of God's embodiment is all around. Each tree is an image of the Tree of Life. Each tree is newly present as a communicator of the life-giving presence of Christ in the world.

When I begin to experience the created world not as something useful but as "charged with the grandeur of God,"[130] as Gerard Manley Hopkins puts it, it is then that my orientation to the world is transformed. I think twice, for instance, about clear-cutting a forest for materialistic ends because I know that so doing reduces the natural world to a utility for which it was never intended. At the same time, I can cut a single tree down to build a dining table for our family, because this accords with the life-giving purpose of creation. When I wonder about God's presence in the natural world I am opened to the *natural nature* of each created thing and how I can turn *with it* toward Christ. I can also see the many ways that we turn created life away from Christ, reducing the natural world to consumable products for profit or undue gain.

The natural world calls me to consider the purposes of God. It urges me to contemplate God anew, and the human tendency to objectify or use people, places, and things to my own selfish ends. Seeing God in the mystery of creation begins with seeing Christ in the incarnate mystery of Holy Eucharist. As wonder is the beginning of philosophy, the Eucharist

---

130. Gerard Manley Hopkins, "God's Grandeur," in *Hopkins Poetry and Prose* (New York: Alfred K. Knopf, Inc., 1995), 14.

is the beginning of theology.[131] When we attend to Christ in the simplicity of bread and wine we will be given to attend to the presence of God in all people, places, and things. The mystery of *God with us* urges us to be perplexed. Yet Christian wandering gives way to wondering about God. And when we are curious about God, we will be all the more curious about each other and our environments, turning toward Christ in all people, in all things.

---

131. Alexander Schmemann, *Introduction to Liturgical Theology*, trans. Asheleigh Moorhouse (Crestwood: St. Vladimir's Seminary Press, 2003), 17.

CHAPTER 22

Turning to Christ in Creation

Christian action is therefore being taken up into God's action through grace, being taken up into God's love so that one can love with him.

Hans Urs von Balthasar

We have seen in the writings of the apostle Paul how life as the body of Christ is intended to pattern our interactions with others in such a way that we reach out to all people as if reaching out to God. What is less obvious is the importance and need for understanding that following Jesus is inseparable from how we relate to all of creation. Just as my reconciliation with God is bound up together with being reconciled with my neighbor—"forgive us our sins *as* we forgive those who sin against us . . ."—likewise is my attunement to the way of Christ inseparable from how I relate to creation and employ its resources.

Christians will often talk about money, how we give, spend, or save. John Wesley once said, "Save much. Spend little. Give a lot."[132] However

---

132. John Wesley, "Sermon 50: The Use of Money," in *Sermons on Several Occasions, 1771* (Grand Rapids: Christian Classics Ethereal Library).

stingy or miserly some Christians may be, there is a felt sense that we are responsible for our monetary resources and should not treat them frivolously, so to honor God with our wealth. Somehow this often comes up short in relation to the natural resources of the earth. When the oil well runs dry, instead of exploring ways to use less oil or tighten our gas-belts (i.e., fasting), we instead create alternative methods to extract less accessible resources (e.g., fracking), which compromises the integrity of the land and soil beneath our feet. We do the same thing with animals. Our overconsumption of meat has given birth to cattle, pig, and poultry farms that are inhumane, hazardous to our health, and detrimental for the ozone layer.

People who live on or near dairy farms, for instance, experience heightened nitrate and bacteria levels in their water, especially if they are on a well system.[133] This is largely due to the concentration of cows on a single farm. More than 50 percent of milk produced in America comes from only 3 percent of dairy farms.[134] With the consolidation of so many farms, supposedly due to cost and efficiency, not only do meat and animal byproducts have to travel longer distances to get to our homes, increasing our carbon footprint, but we are actually poisoning ourselves and the earth in such a way that our bodies and the soil cannot purify themselves fast enough, leading to any number of diseases and detrimental effects on the planet.

We know, for example, that there is a direct relationship between red meat and processed meat consumption and colorectal cancer.[135] Even so, meat farms are increasing in size and production, not simply due to increased population, but also following increased consumption among wealthier countries. Processed meats especially are linked with any

---

133. Elizabeth Grossman, "As Dairy Farms Grow Bigger, New Concerns About Pollution," *Yale E360*, May 27, 2014, accessed November 7, 2018, https://e360.yale.edu/features/as_dairy_farms_grow_bigger_new_concerns_about_pollution.

134. Ibid.

135. H. Charles J. Godfray et al., "Meat Consumption, Health, and the Environment," *Science*, July 20, 2018, accessed November 7, 2018, http://science.sciencemag.org/content/361/6399/eaam5324.

number of chronic illnesses, diabetes, and cardiovascular diseases.[136] This reality reveals several things. For starters, our desire for greater profits and increased efficiency is stripping our communities of ecologically and locally produced meats. Second, the ability to mass manufacture meat on a global scale has enabled us to consume more than our bodies can sustainably digest, as well as forms of meat that our bodies are incapable of properly digesting. Third, but just as important, the fact that we "know" that these foods are detrimental, especially in large quantities, does not stop us from consuming them; because we enjoy their flavor we ignore the damage they do to our environments and to us.

I want to focus on this last example regarding our habits of life. We have seen that wisdom arises when we have ordered our sensibilities to savor God. Thomas Aquinas argues in the thirteenth century that our ability to reason and understand is always influenced by our appetites. If I do not enjoy the taste of broccoli, for instance, it is difficult for me to understand why it might be good for me. If I crave a hamburger topped with bacon, blue cheese, fried onions, and spicy ranch, with a side of tater tots of course, even though I know the burger is not heart-healthy—or remotely healthy at all—because I enjoy its savory deliciousness I "believe" it's good for me, all the while "knowing" that it's unhealthy. My craving—my appetite—conditions what I perceive to be good, even though what is actually good for me may not be what I desire.

The passions of the body condition my ability to think clearly about anything, whether it is the health of the body, a relationship with a friend or stranger, or anything else. If bodily pleasure holds the reins of my appetites I will struggle to understand what is good. I will struggle to follow Christ.

Aquinas goes on to say that the choices we make, because they are conditioned by our appetites, are actually made before we make them. When I'm at the Village Tavern in my hometown for dinner, before I decide to order that burger described above, I have already chosen to do so based on how my eating habits have conditioned my cravings up to

---

136. Ibid.

that point. It is hard not to imagine eating that particular burger when I am at the tavern. I can even take a step back and recognize that before any of this occurs, the very fact that I choose to go to the tavern, which has the burger I love, is because my desire has "carried" me there. The food I need to eat, and should eat for the good of my health and bank account, is right in front of me at home. But this is not what my appetite calls me to. My refrigerator appears empty because my appetite prevents me from seeing the good that is there.

How we relate to the world around us is no different than our cravings. Just as my appetite is conditioned by the foods I have come to enjoy or eat regularly, likewise is my love and care for the earth patterned by various habits and practices. This is why Ellen Davis argues that our ecological crisis is not a technological problem but a theological one. "Ecology," as Davis points out, is the "study of relationships."[137] Body ecology is the study of how our food relates to our gut, just as bioecology studies the relationship between living organisms and their environments. The earth is not unlike our bodies. If we keep poisoning the world with exhaust fumes, pesticides, and genetically modified vegetation the earth will continue to fight back. The oceans will continue to rise and the hurricanes strengthen as they fight off the cancer that is the human race.

What is important for followers of Jesus, and for the rest of humanity, is to recognize, as Davis points out, that righteousness—right relatedness—is first and foremost an ecological matter. Righteousness in the Old Testament is a matter of just relationship with all of God's creation.[138] *"Righteousness means living in humble, care-ful, and godly relationship with the soil on which the life of every one of us wholly depends."*[139] As Augustine writes in *The City of God*, all of life is a matter of orientation. We either orient ourselves to God and the will of God at work in the world and in the soil, or we self-orient to our own desires. The difference between the two is that self-orientation always looks like

---

137. Ellen Davis, *Getting Involved with God: Rediscovering the Old Testament* (Lanham: Rowman & Littlefield Publishers, Inc., 2001), 185-201.
138. Deut. 16:20.
139. Davis, *Getting Involved with God*, 187, italics original.

people who gather more than is needed. We should recall the Israelites in the wilderness who, after God rains down bread from heaven, were commanded to gather only enough for the day, trusting that the Lord would give them daily bread.[140] In a world of refrigeration and frozen foods one must wonder if we ought to wander for a while without storage to reorient our desires.

Look in your home: does your cupboard and refrigerator reveal a people who trust in the provisions of the Lord, or does it manifest habits of consumption that misconstrue the vision of God? I'm not suggesting that we all get rid of our refrigerators. What I invite us to discern is how our habits of storing up for tomorrow are conditioning our loves. Our material habits manifest what we believe about following Jesus today. Are our homes stored with treasures and supplies for tomorrow, or do they reveal a people ready for resurrection—ready to leave it all behind? We cannot take these realities for granted. Refrigerators, grocery stores, prepackaged foods, meat production and its availability, pesticides, genetically modified plants and animals, and so much more impact how we move about the world and condition how we perceive the world, each other, and God. If we are to connect our dinner tables with the Lord's table, the consumption of our homes with being consumed by the Eucharist,[141] then our orientation to the world and its resources must change—our habits must change.

The ecological crisis impacting the planet is first and foremost a spiritual matter. Until we reorient our habits to the way of Christ, which includes whether and how we use automobiles, how we heat and cool our homes, the clothes we wear, the food we eat and how much of it we eat, as well as every other relationship we have with people, places, and

---

140. Exod. 16.

141. See William T. Cavanaugh, *Theopolitical Imagination: Discovering the Liturgy as a Political Act in an Age of Global Consumerism* (New York: T&T Clark Ltd., 2002), especially "The World in a Wafer," 112-122. See also William T. Cavanaugh, *Being Consumed: Economics and Christian Desire* (Grand Rapids: William B. Eerdman Publishing Co., 2008) for a further analysis of desire and consumption. Additionally, for how our ordered and disordered loves shape our relationships, see James K. A. Smith, *You Are What You Love: The Spiritual Power of Habit* (Grand Rapids: Brazos Press, 2016).

things, we will continue along with the Corinthians in failing to discern the body of Christ. To inhabit the way of love in the world—to be inhabited by grace—means changing our minds about *everything* by moving with Christ in every aspect of human living.

Conclusion

> The Eucharist is the action of Christ in his body, his action through
> us for the world.
>
> John A. T. Robinson

What we have been describing is the human tendency to separate the spiritual life from the practical realities of everyday life—our tendency to separate the body from the soul. In so doing we become spiritually schizophrenic. Schizophrenic patients often experience a sensation whereby their limbs appear to be disconnected appendages, even robotic or mechanical appendages to the rest of their body.[142] Each limb is a part that is separable from the whole. Without ever realizing it we do the same thing with the world around us. We do not consider ourselves attached to the soil, at least not in such a way that we connect our life with God to how we relate to the earth beneath. We struggle to recognize the interwoven nature of our lives as individuals with the lives of those around us.

To be the body of Christ—to be a people made by Holy Eucharist— we must begin to make explicit the distinct nature of life in Christ as right-relatedness to all things, to all people, and to all places. This is the way of incarnate love. We do not serve the God who remained in

---

142. McGilchrist, *The Master and his Emissary*, 439.

heaven, but the God who came down from heaven[143] and gives life to our bodies.[144] We serve the God who makes reconciliation with others and the earth possible. Reconciliation, however, this way of incarnate love, is first and foremost a movement. It is a reorienting of desire. Only by reorienting our bodily desires can we begin to change how we think about our relationships. It is time for us to take seriously our *natural nature* as a people inhabited by grace, and to order our lives by the incarnate love of God in Christ. The more we pattern our movements with the movement of Christ, the more we will understand what it means to "lead a life worthy of the calling to which [we] have been called, with all humility and gentleness, with patience, bearing with one another in love, making every effort to maintain the unity of the Spirit in the bond of peace."[145] This bond of peace begins with our feet.

Discussion Questions

1. When you think about the dinner table in your home, do you notice a direct link between this and the Eucharistic table in your church? Does the same hospitality toward the stranger extend to your kitchen?

2. What is the ecology of your home? Where does your food come from? How much oil and gas do you consume? How does the production and waste of your home manifest the goodness and sufficiency of God?

3. How are you learning to savor God in worship, at home, among friends and neighbors? What is the *gout de terroir* where you live and worship?

---

143. John 6:38.
144. Rom. 8:11.
145. Eph. 4:1-3.

PART V

A Rule of Life

"Let Us Go Forth into the World . . ."

Do not judge, so that you may not be judged. For with the judgment you make you will be judged, and the measure you give will be the measure you get. Why do you see the speck in your neighbor's eye, but do not notice the log in your own eye? Or how can you say to your neighbor, "Let me take the speck out of your eye," while the log is in your own eye? You hypocrite, first take the log out of your own eye, and then you will see clearly to take the speck out of your neighbor's eye. Do not give what is holy to dogs; and do not throw your pearls before swine, or they will trample them under foot and turn and maul you. Ask, and it will be given you; search, and you will find; knock, and the door will be opened for you. For everyone who asks receives, and everyone who searches finds, and for everyone who knocks, the door will be opened. Is there anyone among you who, if your child asks for bread, will give a stone? Or if the child asks for a fish, will give a snake? If you then, who are evil, know how to give good gifts to your children, how much more will your Father in heaven give good things to those who ask him! In everything do to others as you would have them do to you; for this is the law and the prophets.

Matthew 7:1-12

CHAPTER 23

Becoming a Spiritual Reservoir

We receive spiritual truth far more by absorption than by exploration.
Evelyn Underhill

The internet has been down all day," she said as I came into the office that afternoon. The parish administrator at the church where I had been serving had tried diligently to adapt to the age of "fast-paced" communication. "Let me know when it's back up. I've got stuff to do in my office anyway," I replied. "Okay," she said, "but I haven't been able to reach Ken all day with the internet being down." "Oh," I said, "are the phones down too?" "No. Phones are working," she said. "Maybe just give him a call?" I responded. "Ha," she said, "I didn't even think to call him."

Habits are hard to break, especially bad ones. Everything around us is working on us all the time, conditioning how we move, feel, perceive, and think. It's hard to remember to pick up the phone and call when our computers and cell phones have us constantly moving our fingers to speak. In the process, our devices physically turn us in on ourselves. Sit down at your computer and notice how your shoulders and back begin to contract toward the screen, even more so when you're looking at your cell phone. Our devices physically close us in on ourselves and if we are not careful we will inadvertently close ourselves off from others. *Perception follows movement.*

Because movement shapes perception we need prayerful practices to help us to (re)imagine more than what's right before our eyes. We also need people who can see what's around us, who can remind us from time to time to stop and look around, perhaps invite us to pick up the phone instead of e-mail. We all live and move within communities of habituation. The question, however, is whether or not we are *aware* that we are being conditioned by many overlapping and often competing worlds—habitats of habituation, if you will.

The encounter with my parish administrator does not describe someone who has never used a phone or couldn't figure it out; rather, it describes the way in which each of our perceptive capacities, in one way or another, condition how we move and thereby relate to others, be they people, places, or things. This leads me to the following conclusion: *If we want to change what we think or believe we must first change how we perceive. In order to change how we perceive, we must first change how we feel. To change how we feel, we must change how we move.* As we will see later, faith, like everything else, begins with our feet.

The Rule of St. Benedict is one of the best places for Christians to begin discerning how movement shapes thought and belief. Benedict, in autobiographical fashion, describes the way of life in the monastery, showing how a monk's actions and speech reveal their habit of life. Benedict also offers prescriptions for attaining Christ through formative habits that make it possible for a person to perceive the world and others as Christ. For instance, the saintly abbot urges the monk to guard his tongue. Speech is important when you live in close proximity with others, especially when you're sharing resources. Interestingly, when Benedict writes about the need to guard one's tongue, he doesn't just refer to what or how something is said. Rather, Benedict invites the monk to silence. The monk, says Benedict, should restrain his speech even when he has something good to say.[146] Silence is the primary form of speech in

---

146. Benedict, *The Rule of St. Benedict*, 31 (XI.1).

the monastery. Why? Silence, more so than speaking, attunes us to the way of humility. This is why Benedict begins his manual for monks with the word *Obsculta*—"Listen." As we saw earlier, *obsculta* means listening with the intent to obey. Listening to Christ is inseparable from moving as Christ.[147] For Benedict, in order to speak as Christ, the monk must first learn how to *move with Christ* in a community of discipline, which gives shape and meaning to his words. This is why listening is emphasized, even when the monk has a word of truth to share.

This seems counterintuitive. Isn't the monk supposed to share what he has learned in scripture, from experience, or from having lived in community for so many years? Will not what he has to share increase everyone else's spiritual vitality? In his magnificent sermons on the *Song of Songs*, St. Bernard of Clairvaux offers keen insight as to what Benedict is getting at here regarding silence, especially being silent even when one is "right" or has something meaningful to say or add.

In Sermon 18 on the *Song of Songs,*[148] Bernard describes the human tendency to pass on spiritual learning without first digesting what one has learned. To help us understand what this looks like, Bernard offers the analogy of a canal and a reservoir. A canal, reminds Bernard, is meant for transporting goods or water from one place to the next; a reservoir stores up water in a single location, and as the level increases it begins to saturate the land around it, providing nourishment to its people and vegetation. We tend, says Bernard, to function like canals. We learn something new or gain some new insight and we immediately want to share it. Our inclination or tendency to do so has only heightened with the rise of social media, where we see something or think something and immediately share it with eight hundred of our closest friends. Often times, however, we don't know what it is that we're sharing. We haven't pondered it enough. We haven't considered how to explain it. We haven't explored its reality for our own life or that of others in order to

---

147. As Kardong has shown, this for Benedict is in keeping with the wisdom found in Proverbs 4, especially as it relates for our purposes to *turning toward* Christ and *moving with* Christ. See Kardong, *Benedict's Rule*, esp. 1-33.
148. Bernard of Clairvaux, *Song of Songs I*, trans. Kilian J. Walsh (Trappist: Cistercian Publications, 1983), 133-139.

adequately communicate its meaning. I hear it or see it, which makes me feel one way or another, and I then share that "feeling" with everyone, whether or not I really understand what it is I am communicating.

It should come as no surprise that our world feels more divided than ever. The speed of our communication—and I use this word lightly—technologies has altered our ability, or altered our willingness, to faithfully discern what it is that we are sharing with the wider world. On top of this, there's no one out there holding us accountable, except for those who disagree with us, and we already know that they're wrong. For this reason, Bernard says we need to function more like reservoirs. When we gain some new spiritual insight or learning we need to sit with it. We need to chew on it, mull it over, and every time we ponder anew the mysteries of *God with us* our spiritual reservoir increases. Eventually, Bernard goes on to describe, through faithful contemplation of spiritual nourishment our reservoir becomes full, and rather than making an effort to tell others what we have learned they begin to see it and know it just by being with us. Our lives come to saturate the lives of those around us, providing nourishment for others in accidental ways. In the process, we are not simply delivering what we have learned, as with a canal. Rather, as a reservoir, our spiritual learning trickles over the edge without depleting our own store of spiritual growth, saturating the soil of others around us and enabling them to likewise become reservoirs of faith for others.

When I am silent, especially when I am silent with something meaningful to say, I learn to listen to God in the everydayness of human interaction and become open to trusting the movement of the Spirit, and not my own will. If I "have to" share my own insights, or if I share these too soon, I may be preventing the spiritual growth of my neighbor who needs to go through similar steps that I went through to know what I have come to understand through obedience to Christ. Or, perhaps my neighbor just needs someone to listen, so that they can hear God in the process.

CHAPTER 24

Moving, Feeling, Perceiving, Believing

Concepts are, after all, chiefly the concentrations of practice and behavior, intent and thought, that give shape and constancy and therefore meaning to our discourse and to our lives.

Paul Holmer

Returning to Benedict, what we've worked through in the previous chapter is the reality that speaking, and silence being a form of speech, is foremost a posture. According to *The Rule of St. Benedict,* the conduct of the monastic, his very posture at the work of God— *opus Dei,* i.e., liturgy and prayer—or laboring in the fields conditions his thinking and, therefore, whether his mind and voice are in harmony when at prayer.[149] It is for this reason that Benedict will say that "you can tell how a monk prays by how he sweeps the cloister." A monk who patiently gathers up each particle of dust and dirt off the floor manifests a corresponding cleanliness and openness before God. The monk who quickly cleans to get done with his task is unlikely to be attentive to Christ when at prayer.

---

149. Benedict, *RB 1980*, Prologue, 45-50.

Let us linger here for a moment and explore a perhaps unlikely guide toward understanding bodily movement and the devoted heart— Constantin Stanislavsky. Stanislavsky was a famous twentieth-century Russian actor and theatre director, and he is best known for his systematic approach to acting, which involves an actor thinking and feeling their role on stage through certain physical movements. For Stanislavsky, the actor is not trying to appreciate the circumstances of the character they are playing; rather, the actor is trying to move as the character moves, embodying the character by being fully present on stage.

In contrast to Stanislavsky is Lee Strasberg, perhaps best known as the father of method acting in America. Strasberg claimed that in order for the actor to play their role well, they must search deep within themselves for an experience in their past that corresponds to the character, and thereby attain a similar emotional state as the character in the play.

The way we might think of these two schools of acting is that Stanislavsky works from the *outside in* and Strasberg from the *inside out*. But what might that difference look like?

Let's say you are playing the role of a person who is ill. If you are Strasberg, you would think back to a time when you were sick, recall all those feelings of dependency, loneliness, and so on, and then perform the role as you lived the experience from before. If you are Stanislavsky, you would not concern yourself with a past experience; rather, you would lie down in bed, groan, and move about as someone who is frail, scared, and alone, and by physically moving about as someone who is frail and dependent, you will come to feel and understand what it means to be scared, what it means to be alone and dependent. If you are playing the role of someone who is nervous or anxious, following Stanislavsky you need not think back to a time when you were anxious or being chased; rather, you would begin by looking over your shoulder continuously, gazing upon strangers with suspicion. In the process, you will begin to take on the anxiety of one who feels as if they are being chased.

It strikes me that Stanislavsky is the more correct, that our bodily comportment is how we attain appropriate ways of inhabiting, not just on the acting stage but also in the world around us. This is key for Stanislavsky because you do not so much come on stage as an actor; rather, you enter the stage as a human being. You enter the stage not as someone who is merely playing a role but as someone who is first and foremost alive. It is not accidental, I don't think, that in contrast to Stanislavsky's method, many students of Strasberg's ended up in years of therapy for acting from their previous and ofttimes deep emotional experiences.

Following Stanislavsky, before ever uttering words an actor must learn to express their character's meaning through eye movements and facial expressions.[150] "My system," said Stanislavsky, "is based on the close relationship of inner with outer qualities; it is designed to help you to feel your part by creating a physical life for it."[151] According to Stanislavsky's method, intuiting the world as one's character is the key to acting. That is, perceiving as the character perceives is the goal of the actor. When actors enjoin themselves to the character in this way, through the habits of the body, they will then be able to speak as their character in such a way that the words make sense—that the words are sensible.

Let's recap: for both Benedict and Stanislavsky, bodily movements condition how we feel. If I move anxiously I will begin to feel anxious. How I perceive is contingent upon how I feel. If I feel anxious I will see others as threats to my well-being. What I believe is intimately bound up with how I perceive the world and others. Can I believe that Christ is the core of another's humanity if I am on guard regarding the potential harm they might cause to my family or me? If Benedict and Stanislavsky are correct, and I suggest that they are, then if I am to seek and serve Christ in all persons it begins with how I move about the world. Faith begins with our feet.[152] Indeed, faith is about guiding our feet and the feet of others along the path of righteousness.

This is the cry of Zechariah at the birth of John the Baptist. The Holy Spirit, as Zechariah prophesies, will work through John, who goes

---

150. Stanislavski, *Creating a Role*, trans. Elizabeth Reynolds Hapgood (London: Methuen Publishing Ltd., 1981), 102.

151. Ibid., 131.

152. See Tadashi Suzuki, *Culture Is the Body* (New York: Theatre Publications Group, Inc., 2015). Suzuki, following Stanislavsky, argues that inhabiting an actor's role begins with her feet. In short, the rest of the body goes with the feet, and everything else follows.

before the face of the Lord to prepare his ways, whereby the dayspring from on high breaks in "to guide our feet into the way of peace."[153] Faith is always a matter of where our feet take us; it always involves attentiveness to the feet of others. If we want to know what we really believe we need only trace our footsteps to find out.

---

153. Luke 1:79.

CHAPTER 25

Praying in 3D

For since the very Author of salvation has redeemed us through obedience, how much more ought we, His servants, to offer the service of humility and obedience.

St. Ambrose

I remember fondly my childhood memories of going to 3D movies. I especially recall watching 3D videos at theme parks, sitting on a bench in front of a large screen with my 3D glasses, watching a roller-coaster ride and feeling as if I were on the coaster. Though my body was completely still, I felt as if I were moving up and down, tossing and turning with the coaster as it jerked from one side to the next. I found myself swaying in all directions, following the movement of the image on the screen. Though still, my body attended to the movement of the coaster. I knew I wasn't on a roller coaster, but I felt like I was moving along the track.

Learning to pray in 3D is a matter of learning to move, both physically and imaginatively, on what we might call a cruciform roller coaster. While there are ups and downs in our life with God, the connection I want to make here is that our prayers are often flat. In her marvelous book, *Everything Happens for a Reason and Other Lies I've Loved,* Kate Bowler describes this flatness—my term, not hers—as a way of relating

149

to God as one who gives material blessings to the faithful and punishes those who are unfaithful.[154] When Jesus describes the matter of blessedness, however, it seems to have little to do with how we often hear the word "blessing" tossed about in modern society.

> Blessed are the poor in spirit . . . Blessed are those who mourn . . . Blessed are the meek . . . Blessed are those who hunger and thirst for righteousness . . . Blessed are the merciful . . . Blessed are the pure in heart . . . Blessed are the peacemakers . . . Blessed are those who are persecuted for righteousness' sake . . . Blessed are you when people revile you and persecute you and utter all kinds of evil against you falsely on my account.[155]

We often use "blessing" or "blessed" with regard to being in possession of some material object or benefit. "I am blessed with good health." "I'm blessed with a nice house, a good job, a wonderful family." Jesus, however, seems to describe the life of the blessed as those who are exhausted, depressed, humble, gracious, and peaceful. Blessing is not a possession; it is an orientation. Blessedness is a posture.

Interestingly, the Hebrew word for blessing is דָּרַךְ (barak), which means to kneel or bow down. Some have argued that the Sermon on the Mount, this series of "blessings," is autobiographical, that Jesus is referring to himself. In this sense, to be blessed is to be a blessing. To be a blessing is to be as one

> who, though he was in the form of God, did not regard equality with God as something to be exploited, but emptied himself, taking the form of a slave, being born in human likeness. And being found in human form, he humbled himself and became obedient to the point of death—even death on a cross.[156]

It should come as no surprise, then, that the Greek μακάριοι (makarioi), from which we get "blessed" or "happy," is not a mere

---

154. Kate Bowler, *Everything Happens for a Reason and Other Lies I've Loved* (New York: Random House, 2018).
155. Matt. 5:3-11.
156. Phil. 2:6-8.

possession of riches or good health. This is a gross reduction. *Makarios*, rather, is more along the lines of being unaffected by the changes and chances of the world due to an overwhelming sense of peace and happiness within. To put it simply, to be blessed is to be "dead to sin and alive to God in Christ Jesus."[157] As St. Irenaeus puts it, "The Glory of God is man fully alive." To be blessed—to be dead to the world and alive to Christ—is to assume a posture of humility, the posture of Christ. It is to relate to God and everyone else, including the world, as one who washes feet.

A two-dimensional prayer life is one marked by an all too casual relationship with God focused on my own needs and desires. A three-dimensional life of prayer is one marked by kneeling and intercession for others and the world.

Aristotle rightly said that "we become just by performing just acts, temperate by performing temperate acts, brave by performing brave acts."[158] To become humble we must perform acts of humility. The principal act of humility is washing feet.[159] Jesus tells the disciples after washing their feet that they need to wash each other's feet, going on to say that "I have set you an example, that you also should do as I have done to you."[160] Interestingly, after he washes the feet of the disciples, telling them they must do the same and reminding them that a follower is not greater than their leader,[161] Jesus then says, "If you know these things, you are blessed if you do them."[162] Again, this begins with *obsculta*, listening with the intent to obey. To serve as Christ is to serve one another, attending to Christ in each other—*obeying* Christ in each other. Washing feet and obedient listening are inseparable in the life of grace.

As with the Sermon on the Mount, Jesus uses the same Greek word μακάριοι (*makarioi*) to tell the disciples that they are blessed if they know

157. Rom. 6:11.
158. Aristotle, *Nicomachean Ethics,* trans. H. Rackham (Cambridge: Harvard University Press, 1999), 73 (II.1.4).
159. See John 13.
160. John 13:15.
161. John 15:20.
162. John 13:17.

they are followers *and* if they wash the feet of others. Accordingly, to know that one is a follower of Jesus is to wash feet. If we do not wash each other's feet, can we know ourselves to be followers of Christ? Can we inhabit the way of the cross, the way of humility, the way of blessing, apart from getting on our knees—*barak*—and thereby becoming a blessing to others? If we do not wash feet, will we be able to hear what the Spirit is saying to the churches?[163]

Søren Kierkegaard, not unlike St. Benedict, refers to this dynamic as manifesting, through the performance of an action, the love of Christ.[164] To wash another's feet, for instance, is an act of humility that makes manifest the humility of Christ. Kierkegaard himself goes a step further, arguing that when we perform an act of love in a way that imitates the love of God we are not working to make love known but, rather, we are working "to make love capable of being recognized."[165] That is, how I relate to my neighbor can either open or close them to the love that is constantly being made known in the world. How I move should make it easier for others to see the love of God that is already in our midst. I am not making love present; rather, I am involved in faithful actions that direct the attention of others away from myself toward the presence of love in the world.

This is what it means to pray in 3D, though we might as well call it 5D for our five senses or 6D for the senses plus the spirit. Prayer and posture are inseparable. To help flesh this out ever further, we return now to the monastery—to the place where the relationship between prayer and posture are, perhaps, clearest in the modern world.

---

163. Rev. 2-4.
164. Søren Kierkegaard, *Works of Love*, trans. Howard and Edna Hong (New York: Harper & Row Publishers, 1962), 30-31.
165. Ibid., 31. For an interesting and further engagement with Kierkegaard on this manifesting of divine love, see Harris Bechtol, "O My Neighbors, There Is No Neighbor," *International Journal of Philosophy and Theology* (London: T&T Clark, forthcoming 2019).

CHAPTER 26

Inhabited by Habits

To be a Christian is a qualification of being, of the whole of a man's being, and the more he opens himself to it, the more completely will it inform and transform all his faculties, including his intelligence.

Josef Pieper

There is a German saying that has carried over into many cultures: *Kleider machen Leute—The clothes make the man.* Similarly, there is a French proverb that arises out of the monastery that counters this: *L'habit ne fait pas le moine—The habit doesn't make the monk.* The phrase comes to us in English as *You can't judge a book by its cover.* When St. Benedict describes the kinds of monks roaming about Europe in the sixth century, he describes some who attempt to live a life by their own rule, rather than living under the discipline of a spiritual master. The Sarabaite, for example, says Benedict, is a "detestable kind" of monk. "In their works they still keep faith with the world, so that their tonsure marks them as liars before God."[166] In other words, *the habit doesn't make the monk.*

Our world has been plagued with one scandal after another regarding wayward priests and bishops whose dress and office mark them as

---

166. Benedict, *The Rule of St. Benedict*, 22 (I.7).

liars before God. Benedict suggests that such persons are liars because what they wear and how they live and pray are at odds. I have met many priests and bishops who enjoy playing dress up a little too much, covering themselves with lace and other clerical paraphernalia. I also believe that a little pomp is good for the church, so long as it does not become pompous. As one who wears a cassock most places, I also think it's important for clergy to be noticeable, even if we are not to "stand out." The breakdown, however, occurs when the movement of the body is in conflict with the way of the cross and the *natural desire* of the soul.[167] Humility, that is, has less to do with humble clothing than it does with a humble posture.

In our home, Amanda is the humblest of us all. I know this because she washes more dishes than I do. Washing dishes is one of my least favorite things to do. I have eczema. It came about when Aydah was born. I blame her. I've managed to rid my body of dryness over the years, with the exception of the palms of my hands. In winter I look like I have stigmata. Eczema means washing dishes is not great for my skin, and it's a good excuse for my not doing them. When Amanda asks if I will, I make the kids wash them. I don't feel as if washing dishes is beneath me in any way, but eczema is a convenient excuse for me to keep my hands from the monotony of such a task.

In *The Rule*, Benedict talks about washing dishes in the monastery. He does so by connecting the dishes of the Lord's table with every pot and pan in the monastery. Indeed, says Benedict, the monk is to "regard all utensils and goods of the monastery as sacred vessels of the altar."[168] Everything is an extension of the incarnate way of Christ. One of the first lessons we learned in "priest's school," not to be mistaken as preschool, despite the many similarities, is that the presence of Christ in, by, and through the Eucharist means that we do not simply whisk the dishes away after everyone has received communion. With utmost care the priest, deacon, and acolytes assist one another in cleaning the paten, chalice, and everything in between such that every crumb and droplet is consumed. If there is too much to consume, it is to be reserved. If there

---

167. See chapter 2.
168. Benedict, *RB 1980: The Rule of St Benedict* (Collegeville, MN: The Liturgical Press, 1981), 31.10.

is too much to reserve, it is to be poured or buried in the ground. Why? Because the presence of Christ mysteriously communicated through bread and wine is mingled with these earthen vessels and they are not to be casually discarded. Christ is bound up together with the bread and wine, consecrating those who gather at the Lord's table, all for the life of the world. This means nothing is to be wasted and all is to be handled with utmost care, for it is Christ that we handle.

This careful attention to Eucharistic vessels is fairly easy to honor, even for more Protestant-leaning persons. Recognizing the dishes in our home as implicated in Christ's body is less easy, especially with plates and utensils well-worn through much use. Yet Benedict suggests precisely that the way we treat the ordinary vessels of life bears witness to what we really believe about God. It makes known how well the movement of the liturgy is giving shape to my ordinary movements in the world. Our treatment of what is common makes manifest what we understand our relationship with others and the world to be. If our careful attention is given only to that which is obviously a portion of God's active presence, we lie, says Benedict, and betray the trust of God.

How we wash the dishes at home is inseparable from our life of prayer. One can hear in the background Jesus's teaching to the disciples: "Whoever is faithful in a very little is faithful also in much; and whoever is dishonest in a very little is dishonest also in much."[169] The connection we are to make here is not the value of the chalice over the pot, or to somehow equivocate the meaning of the two; rather, faithful attention to Christ is a matter of attending to all things and all people with the same level of attention and the same level of concern that we have for Christ. If the love and care we show toward the things of God in church and at liturgy are not saturating the soil of our home, offices, and everywhere else we live and move, it is only because we are still functioning as canals for Christ. It means we need to slow down and become reservoirs. Otherwise, our faith will become unsustainable, and will dry out even while bearing witness to some goodness about God.

---

169. Luke 16:10.

Perhaps an unlikely connection to this careful attention is the parable of the Good Samaritan, specifically Jesus's claim about what it means to be a neighbor. We learn in Luke 10 that a man is left for dead on the Jericho Road. A priest and a Levite both pass him by, going out of their way to avoid the man. What is implied by the parable is that the priest, Levite, and the man lying on the road are all Jews—they share a common ethnicity or nationality. It is the immigrant from Samaria, however, who comes along and notices the man, picks him up and cares for him. In telling the parable, Jesus is responding to a question posed by a young lawyer. When Jesus finishes the story, instead of answering the lawyer's question, "Who is my neighbor?" Jesus responds with a better question: "Which of these three was a neighbor to the man who fell into the hands of robbers?"

The connection between the tools of the monastery, the vessels of the Lord's table, the dishes in our kitchens, and the meaning of "neighbor" in the parable is this: it is not what we see before us that is to determine how we extend care, be it a person, place, or thing; rather, it is the vision of Christ shining forth from the lamp of our eyes that opens us to see all things as involved in the movement of God in the world, to greater and lesser degrees, but no less involved.

"Neighbor" is inseparable from the corresponding actions of my body. Bodily movement conditions how we understand the meaning of our words.[170] Ian McGilchrist has shown how the movement and gestures of our hands are uniquely related to speech. For instance, the words we use to say that we know or understand a person, place, or thing are words such as com*pre*hend, im*press*ion, ex*press*ion, in*tend*, con*tend*, pre*tend*. These words are linked with the Latin *tendere*, "to reach with the hand."[171] To understand is to *grasp* it. Owning this is integral to understanding—grasping—what it means to be a neighbor.

Daniel Miller has also shown that the description of neighbor throughout scripture is a matter of our orientation to God, other

---

170. McGilchrist, *The Master and his Emissary*, 111-115.
171. Ibid., 112.

humans, animals, and the soil.[172] The whole reason for resting on the Sabbath, argues Miller, is to reorient us, the animals with whom we work the land, and the land itself to God. If we do not pause and rest from our labors we will ruin the land, the animals, and ourselves. In being oriented to God for the purposes of God, our neighborliness toward all God's creatures can transform the whole of creation—humans included—into neighbors, just as the Samaritan was a neighbor to the indigent man left for dead, who became his neighbor in the process.

Our movement toward God reorients the world to God. In this way we become "Christ-bearers" in the world.[173] As the Virgin Mary, the *theotokos,* bears God to the world, we bear the world, as Christ, to God. We become *christotokos,*[174] as St. Ignatius puts it, or, in the words of John Chrysostom, "little Christs." When oriented to the way of Christ in the world we become active bearers of an agency that is not our own.[175] We are inhabited by a movement—the grace of God—that at once precedes us yet proceeds from us. Yet the God who is with us will not impose the way of incarnate love upon us; rather, in proportion to our participation in walking in the way of Christ, the Spirit works the work of God in us.

Father Isaac is the pryor at the Abbey of the Genesee in Piffard, New York. I often ask him each year to speak with confirmation candidates about the life of prayer. I find it helpful for young people to learn about prayer from someone who prays no fewer than six times a day, and that only includes set observances of the Hours. On a recent trip to the abbey with three teenagers and their parents, Father Isaac began discussing the way of prayer in the monastery as analogous to a tree and how it affects the surrounding environment. A tree does many things. It shades from the sun; it provides oxygen; it reduces water evaporation; and

172. See Daniel Miller, *Animal Ethics and Theology: The Lens of the Good Samaritan* (New York: Taylor & Francis, 2012).

173. Cyril of Jerusalem, "The Mystagogical Lectures," IV.3, *The Works of Saint Cyril of Jerusalem*, trans. Leo P. McCauley and Anthony A. Stephenson, vol. II (Washington: Catholic University of America Press, 1970).

174. Ignatius, *Epistle to the Ephesians,* I.6; Cyprian, "Letter XVI," in *The Letters of St. Cyprian of Carthage*, trans. G. W. Clarke, vol. I (New York: Newman Press, 1984).

175. See Williams, *Edge of Words*, 111.

much more. Father Isaac highlighted for us, however, how trees purify the air. Trees remove toxins from the air and, as if exhaling, breathe into the atmosphere clean, pure air. An acre of trees, for instance, absorbs enough CO_2 to offset the exhaust emissions produced by a car that travels 26,000 miles in a year; an acre of trees also provides enough oxygen in a year for 18 people.[176] Trees are pretty amazing. We should probably stop cutting so many down.

Father Isaac went on to connect this with the life of prayer in the abbey. "The monastery," said Isaac, "takes in the toxins of the world around it and exhales clean air." Liturgy, prayer, and the life of love shared in community with others—the Church—is to similarly absorb the toxins of fear, selfishness, and hate and to exhale faith, hope, and love into the wider community, reorienting the desires of all toward the way of incarnate love. This absorption of toxins and exhaling of clean air extends well beyond the monastery. It is the path of every follower of Christ. When we give ourselves to the movement of God in the world— to the liturgy of Christ continually occurring in our midst—we become divine filters, as it were, absorbing violence, hate, and suffering of all kind, so that others can imagine more than they experience in a world of disordered loves. Without practices that orient us to the life of grace, we will find ourselves returning violence with violent acts of our own and hate with hateful speech from our mouths, or suffering by injuring others, even in accidental ways. We need habits and practices of peace if we are to absorb the evil and sin of this world and put an end to the vicious cycle of violence and fear.

---

176. "Top 22 Benefits of Trees," *Tree People*, January 26, 2018, accessed November 10, 2018, https://www.treepeople.org/tree-benefits.

Conclusion

Listen and understand: it is not what goes into the mouth that defiles a person, but it is what comes out of the mouth that defiles.

Matthew 15:10b-11

To be inhabited by grace, this way of incarnate love, is a matter of renewing the world through our own bodily habituation toward God, others, and nature. It is about becoming divine filters, whereby we take on habits and practices that absorb the toxins of the world, so that what comes out of us gives life and does not further pollute the good of created life. When we are oriented by faith, hope, and love—when we are turned toward Christ—what we take in will not compromise the grace at work in us.

We are always taking in the toxins of our environments; this is an inevitable reality of living in the world. However, if what comes out of us is not to defile,[177] our hearts must be oriented by prayerful habits that enable us to faithfully respond, rather than anxiously react, to the needs of the world. Otherwise, we will simply come to mirror the fear and anxiety of a broken world.

So, how do we become divine filters? In the section that follows, I offer some expected and unexpected examples of how we might reorient our passions to the movement of God in the world—to the way of

---

177. Matt. 15:10-20.

incarnate love. Some of these will seem obvious, others less so, but they will hopefully enable you to reconsider how your current movements and postures may be keeping you from the love, joy, and peace of Christ and how you might reorient your life to the way of incarnate love. Some will not connect with your own life directly; they are examples of how we might begin to rethink the ordinary as integral to the spiritual life and learn to perceive the world as Christ.

Discussion Questions

1. Consider your own life. When you gain understanding and insight, do you ponder its meaning? Do you "chew the cud," as it were, and inwardly digest what the Spirit is saying? Or do you hastily and haphazardly share insights as if posting an image of your dessert on Instagram?

2. When you think about your local church, how is it becoming a spiritual reservoir for the community? Is your church doing mission work modeled on a canal system, or are you growing spiritually together in such a way that the lives of parishioners are saturating your environment as a reservoir of incarnate love?

3. How well do you "sweep the cloister?" How interwoven are your life of prayer and your everyday movements? How attentive are you to God in the smallest of routines? How might you begin to reorient your life toward Christ one practice at a time?

PART VI

Postures of Perception

You will know them by their fruits. Are grapes gathered from thorns, or figs from thistles? In the same way, every good tree bears good fruit, but the bad tree bears bad fruit. A good tree cannot bear bad fruit, nor can a bad tree bear good fruit. Every tree that does not bear good fruit is cut down and thrown into the fire. Thus you will know them by their fruits. Everyone then who hears these words of mine and acts on them will be like a wise man who built his house on rock. The rain fell, the floods came, and the winds blew and beat on that house, but it did not fall, because it had been founded on rock.

Matthew 7:16-20, 24-25

CHAPTER 27

Roasting Coffee with Jesus

> Now, we face a postmodern wrinkle: we're foraging as often as
> not on unfamiliar ground. We're perpetual tourists, grabbing and
> eating, searching and moving. We revel in our sheer ability to move
> and yet we are somehow surprised and even distressed by the
> burden of it all.
>
> Maggie Jackson

I began roasting my own coffee about two years ago. I roast my coffee daily each evening, just enough for the next morning. When I brew my coffee in the morning, I brew only one cup at a time; I never make a pot of coffee anymore. This process of roasting and brewing has had an interesting effect on my sensibilities. It has become something of a centering discipline that reorients me in the evening and prepares me for the day ahead.

I've been roasting my coffee in the garage over an open flame, which means I am sitting in one place doing one thing for about ten minutes. In the morning, I grind the coffee beans with a hand grinder, and I use a specially made coffee kettle to pour 205°F water over the coffee grinds, through a hemp filter. All in all, this takes about five to seven minutes to brew a cup of coffee in the morning. Again, these are periods in which, because of the process involved, I am only doing one thing. My attention is completely focused on roasting the beans and preparing a cup of coffee.

Sometime in January, the cold weather of western New York moved my roasting indoors. I began using our toaster oven to roast the coffee beans to avoid sitting in the garage, which is not heated. The coffee still tastes just as good. The beans are actually more evenly roasted, as they are equally exposed to the heat, whereas the open flame is less predictable. Nevertheless, I noticed something almost immediately: when I use the toaster oven to roast the beans I do not have to be as attentive to the beans or the temperature. I can set a timer and come back in ten minutes, ready to pull them right out of the oven. Also, during these ten minutes, instead of gathering my thoughts from the day or reflecting on encounters I've had with others, I've found myself working on other tasks, whether it's getting dinner ready, finishing up odds and ends at work, or just doodling around on social media or the internet. The "freedom" of the toaster has enabled me not to be less distracted but *more* distracted, compelling me to neglect the centering practice of roasting coffee by hand. I even recently began cheating with grinding the beans, breaking out my electric grinder, which again saves me very little time—about a whole minute. Still, it's time that I become distracted with other tasks.

I quickly returned to roasting in the garage, wearing a jacket and gloves, and grinding my coffee by hand, recognizing the ramifications more modern methods had on my sensibilities. It also makes a difference in how I enjoy my morning coffee, which I can't get anywhere else. Efficiency is more often than not ineffective. Washing machines, for instance, do not save time. We simply work more so that we can buy more clothing, knowing that we no longer have to wash our clothes by hand. In the process, we become decentered, filling our time with distractions or more work, making it harder and harder for us to attend to relationships, reflections from the day, and more. We need centering practices where we learn to do one thing at a time. When we learn to do this we will also learn how to be present with the people in front of us, rather than being, as Sherry Turkle says, "alone together."[178]

For instance, by roasting my own coffee I have become more attentive to where coffee is sourced, how much of it I drink, and the intricate flavors of each coffee bean region. I only altered my coffee intake and only began tasting the hidden notes of the beans after changing my orientation to the coffee bean itself. Reorienting myself to coffee as a roaster had unexpected side effects that have changed my life for the better. I did not anticipate becoming more centered as a person. I was not trying to be earth conscious in any way. My goal was not to consume less coffee. Nevertheless, in becoming attuned to the coffee roasting process and the intricacies of each bean and region I have inadvertently altered my habits of life in such a way that is more life-giving for myself and others.

Remember when you were researching that subject in college or high school and you stood among the library stacks, looking for the book you had searched for in the catalog? While you stood there looking for your book, homing in on letters and numbers, you began to notice the titles next to your book. You went to the shelf to grab one book and perhaps came out with ten. At least that's what usually happened to me. It was not unusual for me to go to the library for a particular book and end up leaving without it, instead taking several of its neighbors I discovered roaming my fingers along the bindings in search of the first one.

Spiritual practices are a bit like my experience roasting coffee and finding books on the shelf. It begins with one practice, usually quite simple, which takes on a life of its own, centering us in unexpected ways, revealing things we thought we knew about ourselves and God. Thus we grow newly to *know* in our bodies after much practice. The way of incarnate love is not simply about reading scripture and praying prayers every day. It's really about an attunement in all things to the movement of God,

---

178. Sherry Turkle, *Alone Together: Why We Expect More from Technology and Less from Each Other* (New York: Basic Books, 2012).

even in something as small as a coffee bean. After all, Jesus used a mus-
tard seed, which is far smaller. Through practice we attend to creation
in such a way that we learn to savor God. Wisdom is about ordering our
palates—our bodies—before it's about learning the meaning and history
behind the Nicene Creed.

CHAPTER 28

Riding in the Car with Jesus

Silence is the sign of real contact with the spiritual world.
Meditations on the Tarot

One of the most hidden vices in modern culture is the need for control. We fear losing our power. We surround ourselves with devices that make us feel more in command. We exert power over others and manipulate situations in order to maintain control over a decision or event. Churches are filled with management-minded people. I sometimes wonder if people get involved in a local church because they've lost control everywhere else, and because churches are in desperate need of people to take charge of various ministries, we overlook their need to direct. After all, it keeps me from having to deal with it.

I am not exempt from the felt need to control. In my vocation as a priest, I serve on numerous committees and boards, I travel across the diocese to visit churches and colleagues, I travel to homes and hospitals to visit parishioners, and I do most all of this by car. Automobiles may be the single most mind-altering tool in American culture. And every time we get behind the wheel of our cars they continue tightening their grip on our imaginations.

Think about the last time you sat in the passenger seat of a car with someone whose driving sensibilities differ greatly from your own.

Regardless of how well they were actually driving, you became more anxious than usual because it was not your hands on the wheel. We see things differently from the passenger seat. The stop sign or traffic light appears to approach much faster, or perhaps much more slowly, than it does when we're driving. The car in front seems much closer. The car moves much faster or slower. The car in the next lane appears especially close, and you want to say, "Why are you taking this turn so fast? We're not in a race!" What "feels" like it's happening is perceived to be happening because we're not in control of the vehicle's speed or direction.

Amanda and I have totally different driving sensibilities. She's an overcautious driver and I'm a good driver. Okay, I'm much more aggressive, but I don't speed like she does down the interstate. I simply make faster stops and starts and I'm constantly testing how fast our car can take that corner. Yellow speed limit signs are suggestions. White speed limit signs are 10 percent lower than the patrol officer expects you to drive. I tend to make recommendations to her when she's driving that I'm almost certain she finds helpful. When I realized how often I was doing this I decided to keep my mouth closed while in the passenger seat. Although my need to control sometimes gets the better of me, the practice of being out of control in this routine situation has had immense impact on my spiritual life.

By opening myself to sitting with what is causing my anxiety, I began a process of discernment that has borne much fruit. Not only can I ride down the road and just enjoy being in the car with Amanda, I have begun to be less concerned about the unforeseen events that happen each day. I've learned to alter my expectations of others, my expectations of what I think needs to happen. I haven't lowered the bar, nor do I anticipate the worst. Rather, I've learned to just be open to whatever and whoever is there. I've determined to be attentive to the people, places, and things that I encounter. I now find myself walking away from hospital visits thinking, "Well that was interesting." Or, "That was better than I could have imagined." Or, "I know not to do that again." When something I have said in a homily or in passing rubs someone the wrong way I do not feel the need to defend myself or make excuses; rather, I stop, apologize, and ask the other person to help me understand what I could have done differently. In other words, I avoid trying to manage or control the situation; instead I move with the reconciling grace of God in our midst and work constantly to make it recognizable for others.

When he encourages a life of asceticism for followers of Christ, Maximus Confessor is quick to remind that asceticism does not by itself create virtue, "but merely manifest[s] it."[179] Our actions do not create grace, love, or virtue. Our actions make the way of love and grace noticeable and recognizable. By giving ourselves to the way of incarnate love in each and every ordinary encounter of life, we make manifest to others the grace that God in Christ has made manifest to us.

Sitting relaxed in the passenger seat is a Christlike posture. It's a posture of humility. When our fear and anxiety take over, our desire for control kicks in. To remove distress and panic from our lives we must take on a posture of humility toward others. When we do this with the small things, as in being a silent passenger in the car, we reorient our senses to trust in God.

Liturgically, one of the movements that denotes our trust in God is making the sign of the cross upon our bodies. This is part of what it means to be "marked as Christ's own." Making the sign of the cross upon ourselves is often associated with Roman Catholic practices of piety, which many individuals feel is not compatible with Episcopal practice. There is also a history of misuse in the church, where doing so supposedly took off a year of purgatory from our loved ones. Like so many things, due to misunderstandings and misappropriations we just stop saying certain words or performing certain actions. In the process, however, we turn faith into something that is separate from our bodies.

This is how languages die, which is helpfully described in Jonathan Merritt's popular book, *Learning to Speak God from Scratch*.[180] We stop using words because we don't know what they mean. We stop using gestures—or never bother to use them—because we do not know why they were made in the first place. On top of that, making the sign of the

---

179. Maximus, "Ambiguum 10," 1109B.
180. Jonathan Merritt, *Learning to Speak God from Scratch: Why Sacred Words Are Vanishing—and How We Can Revive Them* (New York: Convergent Books, 2018).

cross or making bows in a service is often considered "popish," which bears negative connotations for many. Besides, many haven't the slightest idea when to cross themselves during the liturgy. For these and other concerns, some legitimate and others not, after the Reformation Era liturgy became an increasingly excarnate affair. We are left to wonder, in a world longing for incarnate practices that matter, where sports activities and workout groups continue to gain traction, if our disembodied liturgical practices have any connection with declines in church attendance. As language and faith practices are increasingly reduced to words and ideas they cease to relate to how we actually live in the world. An intangible faith is akin to James's reminder that "faith without works is dead."[181] We might find some of these liturgical movements strange or odd, but they're certainly no more foolish than worshiping a God who died on a cross. Bowing one's head when the name of Jesus is mentioned in scripture or throughout the liturgy is only awkward if we don't believe Jesus is the Messiah.

Earlier we noted how vital hand movements are to speech, understanding, and memory.[182] When our bodies and senses are no longer integrated—when tradition is separated from reason—faith becomes abstract and inconsequential to ordinary life. In other words, we remove Jesus from everyday human life. We separate divinity from humanity, which God in Christ has fused together in an "unconfused union," forever making manifest the purpose of human nature as a bearer of divine agency for the life of the world. When we bow our heads at the mention of Jesus's name in worship we are attending with our bodies to the incarnate reality of humanity as a portion of God.[183]

How we move in the world matters. It matters because this is how faith materializes in the world. We know that feeding the hungry is an act of faith. It brings us closer to those in need, which brings us closer to Christ. This is an embodied action. It makes a difference, for instance,

---

181. James 2:26.
182. 1 Thess. 5:17.
183. For a wonderful exposition on human nature, see Rowan Williams, *Being Human: Bodies, Minds, Persons* (Grand Rapids: William B. Eerdmans Publishing Co., 2018).

whether I simply drop food off for someone who is hungry or if I sit and share a meal with them. Both are good; however, one *matters* more. One is more material, more relationally embodied than the next. Likewise, liturgical postures incline us to relate to God as the embodied creatures that we are. Liturgical movements are how the soul rises to the surface of our lives and the truth of our humanity is made manifest, both to ourselves and to others.

This is increasingly hard to grasp in a society where "God" and "Jesus Christ" are name-dropped in casual conversation to denote some sort of startling occurrence, as in "OMG!" Careless invocation of God corresponds to a carelessness about one's life in Christ. There is much to be said for the Jewish reluctance to spell out *G-d*, or to speak the name Yahweh, as calling upon God should never be haphazard. Moving our bodies reverently at the name of Jesus may very well be what is needed to transform our speech, so that speaking God becomes increasingly thoughtful and meaningful rather than careless and trite.

Stretch your imagination. The nature of Christian prayer is all about being a good passenger—being out of control. We often think of prayer as either trying to curry favor with God or some attempt to cope with the difficulties of life. What if prayer is much more than this? What if prayer is a matter of learning to move with Christ down the highways of life? What if we begin to understand prayer as *listening in* on an eternal conversation the Father is having with the Son, whose Spirit opens our ears to hear what God is saying? Being a passenger in this car ride is analogous to the *apatheia* we described in chapter 17. It's neither active nor passive. It is an inhabiting of and being inhabited by a movement that *precedes* yet *proceeds from* us. Our calling as passengers in the Spirit is to lean in with the turns, attending to every contour of the road, taking in the trees, houses, and pedestrians along the way, trusting that God is actually a better driver than we are.

CHAPTER 29

Moving in Closer to Jesus

What we are to have inside is a childlike spirit; but the childlike spirit is not entirely concerned about what is inside. It is the first mark of possessing it that one is interested in what is outside.

G. K. Chesterton

Forgiveness and reconciliation are also postures. At the eighty-seventh diocesan convention of the Episcopal Diocese of Rochester, we held our meetings and liturgy at the Islamic Center in Rochester. Our bishop, the Rt. Rev. Prince G. Singh, has become known as a bridge builder across faith communities, racial divides, and much more. His connections with various religious leaders in the area led to our meetings being held in the gymnasium connected to the mosque. I was initially uncomfortable with this decision, especially as I was on the liturgical planning team. We were asked not to process with a cross, not to sing, and not to have alcohol (i.e., communion wine). All of my Anglo-Catholic sensibilities were being challenged.

As I shared my concerns and asked my questions, Bishop Singh looked at me lovingly, knowing that I did not quite understand where he was coming from. He explained why this was important for our diocese at this time in the history of the world. To which I responded, "You're the bishop."

On the eve of the diocesan convention I read an interview with Bishop Singh in *The Living Church* about the chosen location and the rationale behind it. I thought it was a favorable and balanced article. Just days after our convention, however, I noticed a picture of the article on Facebook from someone in the "Ritual Notes" group, of which I remain a subscriber. The group is a discussion platform for all things liturgy, though it often treats liturgical dress and practices a bit on the precious side, which never fails to be entertaining. However, this particular post was called "Substituting Grape Juice for Wine?" The comments that ensued from the initial post were any number of defamatory claims about our bishop, our diocese, and the Episcopal Church in general. "This is not Eucharist!" remarked one. "I see all sorts of Title IV violations," wrote another. "This is not Christianity!" declared the righteous.

In the aftermath of the convention, which was one of the most moving, decidedly Christian experiences in which I have ever participated, I said to Bishop Singh, "Thank you for encouraging us to hold our convention at the Islamic Center." I went on to tell him in brief about the postings I read on Facebook, and confessed to my bishop that ten years ago I would probably have thought some of the same things about holding services in a Muslim center and not using fermented wine. Sadly, the hospitality shown by our Muslim friends is hospitality I don't always experience from my Christian sisters and brothers.

Before you're ordained in the Episcopal Church most candidates have to take the General Ordination Exams. I aced my exams, save for one question. The question I bombed had to do with whether or not I, as an ordained priest in the Episcopal Church, would permit a Muslim group to hold a prayer service in our local church. The context was that I was serving in a downtown church with few affordable meeting spaces, and a Muslim group had approached, asking if it would be possible to use our space. I argued in my essay that because the church is a Eucharistic space it would not be appropriate to have any non-Christian group using the space for prayer and worship. I waxed eloquently on

Eucharistic theology and quoted Henri de Lubac on how "the Eucharist makes the church."[184] I failed that question.

Theology is all about describing how God orients us to the stranger, to the poor, to the hungry, to the wealthy parishioner, to the suffering, and even to people of other faiths. Theology in the practice of ministry is all about reaching out to Christ in every person, be they Jewish, Greek, Muslim, Protestant, or your mother-in-law. It has everything to do with friendship with God, and when you are friends with God you are friends with everyone God has befriended, which is *everyone*.

Yusef and I had become friends following an interfaith gathering at the Geneseo Interfaith Center. We began meeting for coffee and discussing the similarities and differences between Christian and Muslim beliefs and forms of worship. Yusef and I would eventually bring together our communities of faith for a night of dinner, music, and good conversation. His community lovingly prepared the food with utmost hospitality. Our Muslim sisters and brothers would not even let us clean up the dishes from the night. They organized an assembly line and kicked us out of the kitchen as they washed and cleaned everything, leaving our parish hall sparkling like it never had before.

Sometime in the middle of our dinner, Yusef came to me and said that it was time for *salah*, time for them to communicate with Allah, and that they needed a place to observe *Isha'a*. I was prepared for this. I knew exactly what to say. "Our church is a Eucharistic space. It would not be appropriate to have Islamic prayers in our building." But that's not what I told Yusef, who is my friend. "Come with me," I said, as I led everyone upstairs into the church. As we entered our gorgeous, neo-Gothic-style church with rich stained glass, I asked Yusef, "Will this work?" "It's beautiful," said Yusef. "Where would be okay for us to lay our mats?" he then asked. "Wherever is convenient," I told him. I shared with Yusef that our church faces east, so that he would know approximately where

---

184. Henri de Lubac, *Corpus Mysticum: The Eucharist and the Church in the Middle Ages,* trans. Gemma Simmonds (London: SCM Press, 2006), 88.

to face for prayer toward Mecca. "Thank you," he said as I left them to observe their time of prayer.

When we're looking for Christ in our neighbors it becomes difficult to see division. My friend Yusef, a devout Muslim, needed a place to pray. That's all I needed to know. What Yusef believes about the particular nature of Jesus is not for me to be concerned with. That is not my calling. My calling is to be Christ, and to befriend Christ in others, regardless of who they believe Christ to be.

Yusef and I continue to gather for coffee and conversation. Neither of us tries to convert the other, but we both have been converted. I haven't changed my belief about Jesus being the Second Person of the Trinity and neither has Yusef been baptized. Rather, each of our attentiveness to God in each other, even though we have different understandings about who God is, has brought about an unexpected friendship and mutual understanding that continues to bear fruit. This is the hospitality of Christ. I have witnessed the way of incarnate love in my brother Yusef, and I am grateful to be inhabited by grace with him, even if we speak of this habituation quite differently.

The hospitality of Christ continues to urge moving in closer to those who are "not me," so that we might perceive Christ in others, even if they do not (yet) perceive Christ in themselves. When we move in closer to our neighbors we begin to see more. When we move in closer to those who believe differently than we do, we understand our own faith better. When we move in closer to those whose sexual orientation we do not share, we begin to recognize that each of our experiences reaches well beyond the mind. We are whole persons who are particular, peculiar, and wonderfully different. God, more often than not, is trying to speak to us through our differences, even if we continue to disagree.

At our diocesan convention we used real wine, though it was non-alcoholic wine. We preached the gospel in ways that I have never heard so clear, even though there was no processional cross. We bore witness to Christ, all the while being in a Muslim gymnasium. From the outside it is easy to see this as heretical or unorthodox. From the outside it is easy to condemn and say that we are not of God. They said the same thing about Jesus when he ate with sinners, tax collectors, prostitutes, and the infirm. They condemned Jesus, who tells the story of a Samaritan—a Jewish heretic of sorts—to offer an example of what it looks like to show real faithfulness to the way of incarnate love.

I am suggesting that when we take on a posture of separateness, instead of moving in closer to our neighbors, enemies, or those who differ from or disagree with us, what good are we? "Even sinners love those who love them."[185] If we followers of Christ cannot step across the aisle, break bread with those of other faiths, and listen to those who differ or disagree with us, it is only because we ourselves lack the much-needed faith to wonder about the movement of God in the world. When I am antagonistic toward others, especially those who do not believe what I believe, it is only because I am uncertain about my own belief. However, when I am confident that Jesus is indeed the way, the truth, and the life,[186] I have nothing to be anxious about. I can begin to see God at work in others, even in people of other faiths, because I know that everyone— every single human being—is an image of Christ our Lord. They are no less a portion of God than you and I, and it's time we began moving in closer to extend hospitality to all people as if extending grace to Christ himself, loving the sinner and the saint as Christ loves us.

---

185. Luke 6:32.
186. John 14:6.

Conclusion

Love alone is credible; nothing else can be believed, and nothing
else ought to be believed.

Hans Urs von Balthasar

In *The City of God*, St. Augustine describes the difference between the
"city of the world" and the "city of God." The difference is not that
of two competing realities; rather, the two cities denote two different
orientations of desire, which arise out of two different performances of
power.[187] The *civitas terrena*—the city of the world—names our tendencies toward self-interests.[188] The *civitas Dei*—the city of God—names
an orientation to what is real, the reality revealed in Christ Jesus.[189] In
his *Confessions*, Augustine pushes this further, saying that the life we
live is a question.[190] What I do with my body, says Augustine, how I
move and where I go, is a continuous search for God, as if asking the
people, places, and things I put myself in front of whether they are the
source of happiness. How we order our relationships manifests what
we believe about the source of happiness, goodness, love, and grace. If

---

187. For a very helpful description of Augustine's "diagnosis," see William Cavanaugh,
Field Hospital (Grand Rapids: William B. Eerdmans Publishing Co., 2016), especially
chapter 7.
188. Augustine, *The City of God*, trans. Henry Bettenson (Harmondsworth: Penguin,
1972), 762 (XVIII.2); see also books XVIII and XIX.
189. Ibid., 843 (XIX.1).
190. Augustine, *Confessions*, X.vi.9, p. 183.

I cannot see Christ in others it is not because Christ is not there; it is only because I ask wrongly,[191] as James puts it.

What I have offered is a way to reflect on your own life as a question. What is your posture toward others, toward the places where you live and move, toward creation, including animals and resources, and everything else in between? How do you ask them about God? And how attentive is your life to their response? Do you inhabit this world as one listening for God in all things, in all people? What about your life as a question needs to change? To ask questions such as these is to inhabit the way of incarnate love. When we do so, we will find ourselves, more and more, inhabited by grace.

Discussion Questions

1. If faith really is an incarnate reality, what habits and practices do you need to change in your own life so that your movements are patterned on the movements of Christ?

2. How does "neighbor" as an activity—as a way of being— transform how you might think about your own neighbors in your community?

3. When did you last make time to get to know someone of a different ethnicity or religious background, or who disagrees with you regarding political or social norms? How have you seen Christ in them? How have they seen Christ in you?

---

191. James 4:2.

Epilogue

All profound things and emotions of things are preceded and attended by silence.

Herman Melville

If the Christian life is not to be reduced to lofty theologizing or feel-good emotionalism it must be as ordinary as breathing air and yet as distinct as a culture and a language. This requires a community—the church; it requires practice—liturgy; and it requires that each of these orient the faithful to the peculiar way of incarnate love in the world. It is learning to attend as embodied creatures to the grace of God at work in us, so that we might be attentive to all things as if attending to Christ. This means listening first, seeking to hear with understanding what is offered, whether another person, God, or the beautiful sounds of creation. It means being still, resisting the temptation to be always on the go. This is easier for some more than others, as is silence. Yet stillness and silence call us beyond ourselves and any immediate anxieties or concerns. They reorient us to what is not "me," which in turn opens me to know that "I" am inseparable from others. This reaches beyond personalities, beyond being introverts and extroverts. We are all different. Some have the gift of gab, while others can sit in silence all day long. The question grace calls us to discern is what lies behind our silence or need to speak. Silence and constantly talking are each often due to anxious fears. I'm afraid of what others might think of what I say, so I keep silent. I'm uncomfortable with silence, so I fill the air with words and noise. Both are attempts to control a situation, rather than giving ourselves to others. Yet silence is essential; it is something with which we all must develop comfort.

As you leave this book, I invite you to craft a modest rule of life, but I encourage you to remember some very important aspects of inhabiting a rule of life. First, no one can live a rule of life on their own. We need others who commit to living this life with us. This is why the church is so important. It is the body of Christ in the world. It needs to be the locus of our life of faith, and it must spill over into the rest of our lives, saturating every nook and cranny of our existence. Churches need to develop a way for parishioners to pattern their lives together in Christ. These ways need to be localized and adapted, accessible and deliberate, and we need to hold each other accountable to the people we strive to become.

Families need a shared rule of life as well. Make time for daily prayer at home. It can be as simple as saying the Lord's Prayer together or as complex as the Daily Office. Either way it needs to be something that happens daily. This is no less important for those who live alone. Daily prayer is essential to orienting our hearts to Christ. When it comes to silence and conversation, how will you create spaces for these? One way is to turn off the phones and just be together. Create spaces where devices are not permitted. Resist using multiple screens at a time. If you're watching a movie together, turn everything else off. Be where you are with whom you are with. Ask yourself and each other how various parts of your home are giving life and which ones keep you from being present or from being a family. It's never too late to change a habit. You can remake your bed. You don't have to lie in it as it is. Eating habits *can* change. You *can* stop buying plastic. You *can* drive less, walk more, go outside, write a letter, pick up the phone, turn off the phone, or sit in silence. You don't have to resign yourself to being busy, on the go, or constantly connected. You *can* be present with God, but it will mean making sacrifices that at first seem hard; yet in so doing you will find yourself drinking from the well of grace, giving life to all you encounter along this way of incarnate love. Above all you will come to recognize in all things and in all people the God who mingles divinity with created life and enjoins us to simplicity, participating in the fullness of what it means to be human. For as Maximus Confessor declares:

> by practicing the virtues the body gains familiarity with God and becomes a fellow servant with the soul. God who dwells in the soul uses it as an instrument to relate to the body and through the intimate bond between body and soul makes it possible for the body to share in the gift of immortality. The result is that what God is to the soul the soul becomes to the body, and the one God, Creator of all, is shown to reside proportionately in all beings through human nature. Things that are by nature separated from one another return to a unity as they converge together in the one human being. When this happens God will be *all in all* (1 Cor 15:28), permeating all things and at the same time giving independent existence to all things in himself. Then no existing thing will wander aimlessly or be deprived of God's presence. For through the presence of God we are called *gods* (Jn 10:35), *children of God* (Jn 1:12), *the body* (Eph 1:23) and *members* (Eph 5:30) of God, even "portion of God." In God's purpose this is the end toward which our lives are directed. For this end man was brought into the world.[192]

Amen.

---

192. Maximus Confessor, "Ambiguum 7," in *On the Cosmic Mystery of Jesus Christ*, trans. Paul M. Blowers and Robert Louis Wilken (Crestwood: St. Vladimir's Seminary Press, 2003), 1092B-D.

CPSIA information can be obtained
at www.ICGtesting.com
Printed in the USA
LVHW080702270819
628972LV00025B/8/P